SVKM'S
NMIMS
Deemed to be UNIVERSITY

NMIMS Management Review

● ISSN: 0971-1023 ● Volume: XXIX ● Issue: 3 ● July-September 2021

NMIMS Management Review

● Volume: XXIX   ● Issue: 3   ● July-September 2021

Editor in Chief
Dr. Tapan K Panda

Managing Editor
Dr. Mayank Joshipura

Published by: **Black Eagle Books,** 7464 Wisdom Lane, Dublin, OH 43016
E-mail: info@blackeaglebooks.org | Website: www.blackeaglebooks.org

ISBN: 978-1-64560-216-3
Library of Congress Control Number: 2021947211

Web address: https://management-review.nmims.edu

Editorial

Sustainability – The Future of Survival

We are living in an unequal world. This inequity is created partly by nature and partly by us. With the growth of civilizations, different nations have moved on the ladder at a different pace and it has resulted in unequal rights on both natural and man-made resources. A part of this inequity has come from the way the world is designed by nature. One cannot decide where to be born, which society, faith and religion to follow and the resources to have access to. This is given by nature. If you are born in a land locked nation in an arid zone of Africa, you are bound to be in extreme poverty. Of course, your desire to see the sunnier days in life, to overcome this poverty trap is through your education, migration and entrepreneurial efforts. Growth and modernization of civilization have led to the formation of greater human civilization over centuries but even this growth has brought further inequity in society. In the process of development and growth, nations have fought wars, made pacts and invested globally to have access to resources. Innovation in science and technology has built greater demand for these finite resources.

Greater is the development, higher is the demand on resources leading to an unsustainable world. The human race has been able to drive out other races (making some of them even extinct from the earth) from this competition to have control over the resources. Population growth coupled with development in science and technology has fueled the consumption of finite resources of the world at an unimaginable speed. It seems as if there is no tomorrow and we will end up consuming everything that the mother nature has bestowed on us over billions of years in a couple of centuries. This sheer drive for materialistic pleasure has resulted in an increased concern for the future generations. Policy planners and futurists have started asking questions about the future that we intend to handover to our next generation,

Concern for sustainability is forcing policy planners, governments and business strategists to rework their vision and build a future based on sustainable consumption. People are talking about a symbiotic relationship between people, planet and profit.

https://doi.org/10.53908/NMMR.29030E

NMIMS

NMIMS Management Review
ISSN: 0971-1023
Volume XXIX
Issue-3 | July 2021

Sustainable development is a more complex phenomenon as it has a complex stakeholder structure beginning from an Individual to global governing bodies like UNO. The world population by 2060 is likely to increase by 50%. This explosion will demand a different economic structure, pricing of goods and services, social responsibility and viability of corporations in the long run.The World Bank has also recognized way back in 1992 that environmental degradation has the capacity to destroy societies. Sustainable development is the magical answer to bring a balance in our society despite a debate on the scope, nature and direction of sustainable development (Castro, 2004).

Sustainable marketing is a sub-domain of sustainable development and is based on two domains. Firstly, we need consumer marketing in our world for society's survival and secondly, the excessive consumptive pattern can cut down our societal fabric. Sustainable marketing is a process of planning, implementing and controlling the development, pricing, distribution and promotion that satisfy the consumer needs, organizational objectives and ensure eco-system compatibility (Fuller and Gilleett, 1999). It is the eco-system compatibility that drives the argument about earth's resources being finite and the human race doesn't have a single, monopoly based consumption right over these resources. The governing philosophy in practice is centered around anthropocentrism, classical utilitarian, or human centered ethics. The anthropocentrism is based on growth oriented economic development and earth's resources linked with human progress. There is an open acknowledgement that Western civilization affliction is an addition to material consumption (Singer 2001). This kind of consumption takes us to non-sustainability. There is a counter argument that sustainable development- sustainable marketing will jeopardize our standard of living, individual autonomy and self-identity through limiting consumption preferences (Beekman, 2004).

Biotic egalitarianism or life centered ethics (Rosen, 2000; Singer, 2001) talks about the human and non-human species on biospheric terms. It is the human behavior that constitutes moral significance implications in Western philosophy where civilization is looked upon as a 'ladder of life' and 'value judgement'. So the fundamental question is whose and what values do we follow? Justification of moral judgement is the basis of sustainable marketing (Is not that the question that Erin Brockovich asks in Erin Brockovich (2000) or Danny Archer's questions in the movie Blood Diamond (2006)). Sustainable development analyzes the relationship between the human race and nature (Magee, 2001). The anthropocentric view doesn't value the relationship between human demands related to natural resources. Bond (2005) is of the view that the pressure on earth has almost doubled since 1970s. The consumptive pattern is not sustainable for the future generation. So what kind of policies should be in place for a sustainable world ? (Beekman, 2004).

The angrier side of sustainable development emerges from the radical environmentalism (remember Green Peace Movement and their demonstrations); may have an evolutionary origin with conservatism and utilitarianism; may have emerged as a natural response to the discussion on thinking forums and journals. The three fundamental pillars of sustainable development are: Firstly, the existence of a theoretical base with practical implications; secondly modelling can increase theoretical promotion and operational gateways and thirdly, a spatial framework can be developed for environmental advocacy and management (Robert and Hills, 2002). The domain of sustainable development research focuses on four major areas: ecological, economic, social and cultural. Discipline of sustainable marketing emerges from arguments that earth's eco-system suffers from a consumer driven, mindless consumption drive that has emerged due to population growth, rapid access to consumption capital and massive adoption of consumer centric technology propelling exponential demand for derived goods and services from natural resources.

Unfortunately, we have not been able to develop a business model that favors economic growth as well as sustainable business practices- it is always at the cost of the phenomenon to bring in a desperate debate about the future of the world. In one of the articles published in Wall Street Journal titled 'The Limits to Growth: A Report for the Club of Rome's Project on the Predicament of the Mankind', the authors accept the steam engine of consumption asking for a mindful and retrained consumption (Melloan, 2002). The alternative view point ignores this sensibility and argues that there is enough in the world and earth has a capability to recreate forever arguing that economic and technological interventions are always positive- at least greater good than the preached negatively. However, the demand of consumption is alarming- we are moving from a 6.1 billion population in 2000 to 8.9 billion in just fifty years. This fifty percent growth in population will put huge outflow of earth's material resources (Daniels, 2003).

These alarming growths for resources need to be researched well to find strategies and solutions. There cannot be any other high impact research other than the question of earth's survival. The Neo-Classical theory emphasizes on decision making abilities between firms, maximizing shareholder value and profitability with a weak sustainability approach (Goldstein, 2002; Faucheux, Muir and O' Connor, 1997). It can be argued that capitalism theories have not been able to deliver greater social equity- in terms of poverty reduction, social equity, or equitable access to technology. The invisible hand theory introduces the dual role of economic development and environmental sustainability within a capitalistic system (Castro, 2004). The capability theory has the ability to promote business opportunities through the promotion of horizontal flows like sustainable product design, lean and balanced engineering processes and technological capabilities to promote methods and machines reducing/ controlling pollution (Goldstein, 2002).

NMIMS
NMIMS Management Review
ISSN: 0971-1023
Volume XXIX
Issue-3 | July 2021

Societal actions change when we are confronted with a major concern/threat. So we assume that society's view point towards sustainability will change when we face such adverse situations- but are we are too late for the same and when we arrive at the door of the hell, will the Satan allow us to look back and self-correct? Passmore's 'Chain of Love' principle propagates public sentiment adopting new values that will protect the environment. This principle is based on the emotional tie between generations. It is based on the foundation that as we love our next generation, we will make the world sustainable at any cost.

Economic growth drives consumption and mass consumption which is the antecedent to pollution. So the key focus of research ought to be product, process and machine designs that can restraint wastages. Adoption of Product System Life Cycle (PSLC) can lead to sustainable consumption (Fuller and Gillet,1999) and Material Flow Analysis (MFA) based on Buddhist economics can lead to sustainable consumption (Daniels, 2003). The MFA is like an ecological blueprint with a potential to have a positive impact on the earth.

A new debate has emerged on environpreneurialism. This has three propositions. The first focuses on innovation and technology than regulatory or consumer activism; second, focuses on the adoption of entrepreneurial viewpoint and the third focuses on the coalescence of environmental, economic and social objectives Lyon and Laxwell, 1999). The three major assumptions are one, recognizes that business has a negative impact on the environment and people will seek for products with low environmental impact (Ottman, 2003); sustainable development and marketing are internal driven philosophies guiding business than a business or regulatory decision (Ryan, 2003, Mirvis, 1994) and third, socially responsible business proposition goes well with environpreneurialism (Osterhus, 1997). Let me end with questions that eco-designers are working on to build a business model:

➢ Can two or more functions be put into one product (product convergence)?

➢ Can the product used be rented /shared instead of the product purchased (shared consumption)?

➢ Can low impact material be used (material discovery)?

➢ Can material usage be reduced (lean manufacturing)?

➢ Can water or energy consumption be used (therapeutic use)?

➢ Can **the** product's lifetime be extended (no-replacement demand)?

➢ Can products be reused, remanufactured and recycled (rebirth of products)?

We at NMIMS Management Review would like to open up this discussion on sustainability and work towards building an environment. Social and governmental

NMIMS
Management Review
ISSN: 0971-1023
Volume XXIX
Issue-3 | July 2021

(ESG) framework that will guide the future research. We welcome high impact research papers in this area so that we can put forth a cohesive argument towards sustainable business practices and decisions for a better world.

Happy Reading!

Dr Tapan K Panda
Editor in Chief

References

Beekman, V. (2004). Sustainable development and future generations. *Journal of Agriculture and Environmental Ethics, 17*, 3-22.

Bond, S. (2005). The global challenge of sustainable consumption. *Consumer Policy Review, 15*, 38-45.

Castro, C. J. (2004). Sustainable development: mainstream and critical perspectives. *Organization & Environment, 17*, 195-226.

Daniels, P. L. (2003). Buddhist economics and the environment: material flow analysis and the moderation of society's metabolism. *International Journal of Social Economics, 30*, 8-34.

Faucheaux, S., Muir, E. and O'Connor, M. (1997). Neoclassical natural capital land theory and "weak" indicators for sustainability. *Land Economics, 73*, 528-552.

Fuller, D. A. and Gillett, P. L. (1999). Sustainable marketing: strategies playing in the background. *American Marketing Association Conference Proceedings, 10*, 222-224.

Goldstein, D. (2002). Theoretical perspectives on strategic environmental management. *Journal of Evolutionary Economics, 12*, 495-524.

Lyon, T. P., Maxwell, J.W. (1999). Corporate environmental strategies as tools to influence regulation. *Business Strategy and the Environment, 8*, 189-196.

Magee, B. (2001). *The story of philosophy*. New York, New York: A Dorling Kindersley Book.

Melloan, G. (2002). 'Limits to growth,' A dumb theory that refuses to die. *Wall Street Journal*, New York, A13.

Mirvis, P.H. (1994). Environmentalism in progressive businesses. *Journal of Organizational Change Management, 7*, 82-101.

Osterhus, T. L. (1997). Pro-social consumer influence strategies: when and how do they work? *Journal of Marketing, 61*, 16-30.

Ottman, J. A. (2003). Green marketing. *In-Business, 25*, 31-34.

Roberts, P. and Hills, P. (2002). Sustainable development analysis and policy in east and west – the cases of Hong Kong and Scotland. *Sustainable Development, 10*, 117-121.

Rosen, S. (2000). The philosopher's handbook essential readings from Plato to Kant. New York: Random House Publishing.

Ryan, P. (2003). Sustainability partnerships: eco-strategy theory in practice? Management of Environmental Quality, 14, 256-287.

NMIMS
NMIMS Management Review
ISSN: 0971-1023
Volume XXIX
Issue-3 | July 2021

The Impact of Business Cycles, Stock Market Phases and Crisis on the Value Premium: The Indian Experience

Received: 24 Dec 2020
Revised: 25 April 2021
Accepted: 4 Sept 2021

https://doi.org/10.53908/NMMR.290301

Priti Aggarwal ● **Vanita Tripathi**

Abstract

Purpose :This paper is an attempt to explore the relationship between the value premium and expected stock returns in the Indian stock market and evaluates whether the value premium disappears or not when the different economic conditions (Boom & Recession), market conditions (Bull & Bear) and 2008 Global financial crisis are considered.

Methodology: The annual data of 500 companies belonging to BSE-500 from 1999-2017 was collected and ten portfolios were constructed and sorted using six valuation proxies (P/B, P/E, D/P/, CF/P, S/P and EV/PBDITA). Standard CAPM and Dual beta market model were employed.

Findings: The empirical results confirm that irrespective of market conditions, value stock portfolios surpass growth stock portfolios in the Indian stock market by delivering significant abnormal returns.

Practical implications: The paper holds important implications for asset pricing literature and investors. The higher returns generated by value stocks during the crisis and recession period imply that investors can put faith in the value stocks during times of adversity. The future value of an investment is a function of its present price. The lower the price, the higher the returns will be. Therefore, value stocks are good investments whether it is boom or recession, bull or bear, crisis or non-crisis periods.

Originality: The paper is first of its kind to study the impact of business cycles, stock market phases and crisis on the value premium in the Indian stock market. The paper contributes to portfolio management and asset pricing literature for an emerging market.

Keywords: *Business Cycle, Economic Conditions, Stock Market Conditions, Global Financial Crisis, Value Investing*

SVKM'S
NMIMS
Deemed to be UNIVERSITY

NMIMS
Management Review
ISSN: 0971-1023
Volume XXIX
Issue-3 | July 2021

1. Introduction

Voluminous literature dating as far back as the 1930s great depression (Graham and Dodd, 1934) observes value premium for the U.S. market (Rosenberg, Reid and Lanstein, 1985; Fama and French, 1992, 1993, 2006, 2008; Lakonishok, Shleifer and Vishny, 1994; Chan and Lakonishok, 2004) and other advanced markets of the world like the U.K., Japan and European markets(Chan, Hamao and Lakonishok, 1991; Fama and French, 1998, 2012; Foye, 2016; Garcia, M.T.M and Oliveira, 2018). The value premium is observed when the returns on the value stocks exceed returns on the growth stocks. However, this pattern is not necessarily translated to the developing and emerging markets(Rouwenhorst, 1999; Chen, Petkova and Zhang, 2008; Ebrahim et al., 2014; Cakici, Tang and Yan, 2016; Hu et al., 2018). Studies are not in consensus whether the value premium is permanent and is here to stay (Fama and French, 1998; Athanassakos, 2009; Artmann, Finter and Kempf, 2012) or is short-lived and is gradually fading away(Yen, Sun and Yan, 2004; Leivo and Patari, 2009). However, without testing the robustness for the emerging markets, it is hard to agree with the above notion's universality. The emerging markets have less developed stock markets which have low liquidity and less industrialisation and higher transaction costs with high growth potential and more open for economic liberalisation (Bekaert, Harvey and Lundblad, 2007).Also, differential behaviours of stakeholders in the emerging markets require diverse measures to deal with market information(Reddy, Qamar and Rao, 2019).The motivation of the study lies in the seminal work of contrarian investing(Lakonishok, Shleifer and Vishny, 1994). In this paper, the authors argued "value stocks would be fundamentally riskier than glamour stocks if, firstly, they underperformed glamour stocks in some states of the world, and secondly, these are on an average in "bad" states, in which the marginal utility of wealth is high, making value stocks unattractive to risk-averse investors." Their results demonstrated that value stocks outperform growth stocks in every state of the U.S. economy. In India, studies have provided mixed signals regarding the presence of value effect (Banerjee, De and Bandyopadhyay, 2018; Sobti, 2018; Tripathi and Aggarwal, 2018, 2020). However, none of them investigated the impact of market and economic conditions on the value premium.

The Indian economy differs from the advanced nations on most grounds. Around 50% of the Indian stock market is promoter-owned and is a growing economy with a young population and lower per capita income. At present, India is one of the five major emerging national economies BRICS. According to the International Monetary Fund, 2019, the Indian economy is one of the fastest-growing trillion dollar economies in the world and the third-largest economy by purchasing power parity (7.98% of world GDP). The country ranks as the fifth-largest economy (2935.57 billion$ GDP). The tremendous economic growth experienced by India during the last three decades had

NMIMS
Management Review
ISSN: 0971-1023
Volume XXIX
Issue-3 | July 2021

a spill over effect on the stock market, lending and investment, financial system, and financial stability. The popularity of India as an investment destination can be witnessed by the steep rise in the foreign portfolio investment (FPIs) in India during the last 20 years (2000-01:2.6 billion US$; 2017-18:22.1 billion US$). Interestingly, when the global financial crisis hit the world in 2008–2009, the developed economies like the United States witnessed their economic growth drop to as low as _0.14%, however, India was resilient and showed a positive GDP growth rate of around 3.09% (World Development Indicators, World Bank). Motivated by the past empirical works in the advanced economies and the unique characteristics of the Indian economy, this paper explores the effect of economic conditions (boom & recession), market conditions (bull & bear) and global financial crisis on the value premium in the Indian capital market.

The paper is divided into five sections including Section 1 introduction. Section 2 presents the review of the literature. Section 3 describes the data and methodology used while Section 4 presents the empirical results obtained. Finally, Section 5 presents the summary and conclusion.

2. Review of literature

Several studies have studied the portfolio performance of value and growth stocks when the stock market conditions are factored in. In a study conducted in the U.S. for 1986-2003, the average annual returns of growth stock portfolios were higher than value stock portfolios for all trading frequencies during the rising market. The authors suggested an investment strategy wherein the investor should invest in growth stocks with high P/E during the booming economy and bullish market and in value stocks with low P/E during recession and bear market(Cheh, Kim and Zheng, 2008)high price/earnings (P/E.In a similar study of the U.S market (Arshanapalli and Nelson, 2007), the authors found that value stocks did not perform well as growth stocks during bull markets but surpassed them in bear markets. Value stocks outperformed growth stocks in non-recessionary periods and added to their lead during recessions using the data of January 1962-April 2005.An international study found that the returns for various investment styles such as momentum, earnings variation and leverage are cyclical but the returns for value stocks and growth stocks are not significantly different during expansionary and recessionary phases of the economic cycle in the U.S. (from February 1973 to December 2008), Europe (from January 1997 to December 2008) and Japan (from December 1984 to December 2008) respectively(Beckers and Thomas, 2010)The impact of the Asian crisis on returns to value strategies was studied for four Asian markets by employing the Average Price Level (APL) rank sorting. The study discovered value premium is time-varying and it becomes greater in the post-Asian crisis period across all four countries indicating high volatility during the crisis(Brown et al., 2008). On similar lines, another study

NMIMS
Management Review
ISSN: 0971-1023
Volume XXIX
Issue-3 | July 2021

was conducted for Taiwanese equity data from July 1985-June 2009 covering 1997 the East Asian financial crisis and 2008 global financial crisis and value-based strategies earned significantly excess returns. B/M based value premium increased post the Asian and the 2008 financial crisis(Huang, 2011)"ISSN":"0927538X","abstract":"Using Taiwanese equity data, we find that value-minus-growth strategies (HML.Another study conducted using 1351 Canadian companies' data for 1985–2005 using P/E and P/B recorded a persistent strong value premium for the whole period, which also lasted in the bull and bear markets and recessions and recoveries(Athanassakos, 2009). In this study, the dual-beta market model (Bhardwaj and Brooks, 1993)is used to study the impact of different economic conditions on the value premium. The model has been extensively used for size effect(Kim and Burnie, 2002; Rutledge, Zhang and Karim, 2008; Switzer, 2010; Teh and Lau, 2017)US and UK but seldom used for value effect. This study shall be the first Indian study to examine the economic and market conditions-domestic and international using the dual-beta model.

3. Data and Methodology

Data: The sample data is obtained from PROWESS. It is widely acclaimed financial software of the Centre for Monitoring Indian Economy (CMIE). The sample period runs from June 1999 to March 2017. The BSE-500 index is taken as the Market portfolio. Comprising of the top 500 companies listed at BSE Ltd., this stock market index includes all the major industries in the Indian market. The monthly stock returns are computed using the equation:

$$R_{i,t} = \frac{P_{i,t} - P_{i,t-1}}{P_{i,t-1}}$$

Where $R_{i,t}$ is the return on stock i in period t and $P_{i,t}$ and $P_{i,t-1}$ represents closing price on stock i in period t and t-1.The adjustments of dividends were not made in the returns as dividends were too small in relation to the total returns.

Similarly, market returns are computed using the above equation for BSE-500 equity index values. For risk-free return, implicit yields on 91-days treasury bills from the Reserve Bank of India (RBI) monthly Handbook of Statistics is used (rbi.org.in). This study has employed six valuation criterions and a brief description of all these criteria is given below:

3.1 Price to Book Value (P/B) Ratio

The book equity to market equity(BE.ME) ratio is frequently used to find the value of a company by comparing the book value of a firm's common stock to its market

NMIMS

NMIMS
Management Review
ISSN: 0971-1023
Volume XXIX
Issue-3 | July 2021

value(Loughran and Wellman, 2011; Gray and Vogel, 2012; Gharghori, Stryjkowski and Veeraraghavan, 2013; Pätäri and Leivo, 2017). This ratio is one of the prime ratios considered by investors to evaluate whether the stock's market price exceeds its book value. A high BE/ME ratio may signal that the company is experiencing problems regarding the fundamentals of the company. Conversely, a low BE/ME may signal that investors have huge hopes regarding the prospects of the company (Fama and French, 1992). Following the seminal work (Fama and French, 2007a, 2007b; Athanassakos, 2011), price-to-book ratio (P/B) to sort the stocks have been used.

3.2 Price to Earnings (P/E) Ratio

The Price to Earnings ratio is a market prospect ratio that compares the market price per share with the earnings per share. The lower P/E ratio gives a perception to the investors that they are paying less for earnings and consider it as a cheap stock. Conversely, high P/E stocks indicate that investors believe and expect the company's future earnings are decent and acceptable. The P/E as a valuation measure has been used extensively in the literature (Basu, 1977; Fama and French, 1998; Hou, Karolyi and Kho, 2011; Penman and Reggiani, 2013)

3.3 Dividend to Price (D/P) Ratio

A stock's dividend yield (D/P ratio) compares the dividend per share with the current price of the stocks. The relationship between D/P and returns has been studied extensively (Ball, 1978; Keim, 1985; Ang and Bekaert, 2007). The firms with higher D/Ps are often thought of as a signal that management believes in continuing with their dividend-paying ability.

3. 4 Cash Flow to Price (CF/P) Ratio

Cash flow is the reported earnings with all non-cash expenses such as depreciation and amortization added back. Most of the preliminary studies using CF/P were conducted in Japan (Chan, Hamao and Lakonishok, 1991; Lakonishok, Shleifer and Vishny, 1994) which later got extended to other parts of the world(Gregory, Harris and Michou, 2001; Hou, Karolyi and Kho, 2011).

3.5 Sales to Price (S/P) Ratio

Sales are considered to be more stable(Damodaran, 2012) and unlike earnings and book values, they are difficult to manipulate, therefore, the metric of the Sales-to-Price ratio is increasingly attracting attention in the financial domain(Senchack and Martin, 1987; Bird and Casavecchia, 2007; Gharghori, Stryjkowski and Veeraraghavan, 2013). S/P explained U.S. stock returns better than B/P or size (Barbee, Mukherji and Raines, 1996; Leledakis and Davidson, 2001; Dhatt, Kim and Mukherji, 2004).

SVKM's
NMIMS
Deemed to be UNIVERSITY

NMIMS
Management Review
ISSN: 0971-1023
Volume XXIX
Issue-3 | July 2021

3.6 Enterprise Value-Based Multiples

The enterprise value takes the company's debt into account. Due to the inclusion of debt, enterprise value gives a clear picture of the company. The most commonly used enterprise-based valuation multiples are EBIT/EV(Pätäri, Karell and Luukka, 2016) and EBITDA/EV(Leivo and Patari, 2009; Loughran and Wellman, 2011; Gray and Vogel, 2012)Novy-Marx, and Zhang (2010, and S/EV. EBITDA (Earnings before interest, taxes, depreciation, and amortisation) tells how much cash would be available to the owners to use either for servicing the debt or reinvestment purposes.

Construction of Value-Sorted Portfolios:

Decile portfolios are formed for all the valuation proxies for every year for all the sample stocks. In June end of Year T, companies are arranged in the ascending/ descending order based on the valuation measure under consideration. Subsequently, these arranged companies are split into ten equally-weighted portfolios namely P1 to P10. For these portfolios, equally-weighted monthly excess returns are assessed for the next twelve months (July of year T to June of year T+1).These are referred to as unadjusted returns. The portfolios have been constructed to be equally weighted since they contain fewer estimation errors compared to the value-weighted portfolios(Lakonishok, Shleifer and Vishny, 1994).Further, the three-factor model does a better job in explaining equally weighted portfolios than value-weighted portfolios(Fama and French, 1996).Firstly, the portfolios based on the stock's P/B ratio are formed. P1 is the extreme value stock portfolio comprising 10% of the total sample with the lowest P/B while P10, the extreme growth stocks portfolio comprises 10% companies with the highest P/B. A portfolio VMG is also constructed to assess the economic feasibility of value investment strategy (buying P1 & short selling P10). The portfolios are rebalanced in June-end of every year. Since the portfolios are formed and held annually, the annual holding period begins in July and ends in June. The sample companies are sorted in June of each year beginning in June1999 and this portfolio formation is repeated till June 2016. It is important to specify that the complete data was not available for all companies throughout the study period of 18 years and hence the effective number of companies used in the analysis ranges from 210 to 480. The robustness of the results is checked by five more proxies. The companies were ranked in ascending order for P/B, P/E, and EV/ PBIDTA and in descending order for Dividend yield, Cash Flow yield, and S/P. The returns on the market i.e. BSE-500 index have also been calculated monthly from July 1999 to March 2017. To use the yields on 91-days T-bills, the annualised yields are converted into monthly yields. The Financial Year in India runs from April to March. Nonetheless, the portfolio formation is carried out in June end so that investors can access the complete accounting information of the companies. Generally, there is a deferment in the publication of financial statements. This also helps to avoid the look-ahead bias.

NMIMS
Management Review
ISSN: 0971-1023
Volume XXIX
Issue-3 | July 2021

The Standard CAPM (Capital Asset Pricing Model) has been used to study the value effect (Sharpe, 1964; Lintner, 1965).

Standard CAPM

$$R_{Pt}-R_{Ft}= \alpha_p+\beta_p (R_{Mt}-R_{Ft})+\varepsilon_t (1)$$

Where,

$R_{Pt}-R_{Ft}$ = Excess Portfolio Returns in period t

$R_{Mt}-R_{Ft}$ = Market Risk Premium in period t

α_p = Intercept term and is a measure of abnormal returns

β_p = Beta coefficient that measures the sensitivity of portfolio return to market return

ε_t = Error term.

The intercept (α_p) is Jensen's risk-adjusted abnormal performance measure. (Jensen, 1968). A statistically significant value of α_p indicates the possibility of abnormal returns. The alphas and betas can vary over time because of the changes in the market and economic conditions. Therefore, a dual-beta market model (Bhardwaj and Brooks, 1993) is implemented.

Effect of Economic Conditions: The boom and recessionary periods for the Indian market are obtained from the Federal Reserve Bank of St. Louis. Boom and recession periods dates are given below:

Boom : July 1999-December 1999, February 2003-September 2007, April 2009-January 2011, July 2013-April 2016

Recession: January 2000-January 2003, October 2007-March 2009, February 2011-June 2013, May 2016-March 2017

The following modified dual-beta model is estimated:

$$R_{Pt}-R_{Ft}= \alpha_0+ \alpha_1 D_R+\beta_0 (R_{Mt}-R_{Ft})+ \beta_1 D_R (R_{Mt}-R_{Ft})+\varepsilon_t (2)$$

Where D_R is equal to 1 for recession months and 0 for the boom months. α_0, $\alpha_0 + \alpha_1$, represents excess return, and β_0, $\beta_0 + \beta_1$ represents beta coefficients for boom and recession respectively.

Effect of Market Conditions: For identifying bullish and bearish market conditions, the median return of the market index i.e. BSE 500 Index is used (Bhardwaj and Brooks, 1993). First, the market returns on the index are calculated for every month, and thereafter median market return is computed. The bull phase is the period of

NMIMS
Management Review
ISSN: 0971-1023
Volume XXIX
Issue-3 | July 2021

increasing market returns falling above the median market return and the bear phase is the period of decreasing market returns falling below the median market return. Each of the 213 months is classified as either a bull month or bear month if the market return in that particular month is higher or lower than the median market return to finally arrive at 106 bull months and 107 bear months. The following modified dual-beta model is estimated:

$$R_{Pt}-R_{Ft}= \alpha_0+ \alpha_1 D_B+\beta_0 (R_{Mt}-R_{Ft})+ \beta_1 D_B (R_{Mt}-R_{Ft})+\varepsilon_t (3)$$

Where D_B is equal to 1 for the bull months and 0 for the bear months. α_0, $\alpha_0 + \alpha_1$, represents excess return and β_0, $\beta_0 + \beta_1$, represents beta coefficients for bear and bull markets respectively

Effect of Global Financial Crisis: The global financial crisis 2007-08 originated in the USA as the subprime mortgage crisis soaked liquidity from the global financial system and battered down financial markets across the globe. The crisis period is taken as the period from December 2007 to May 2009 as identified by the National Bureau of Economic Research (NBER). Two dummy variables D_1 and D_2 to account for three periods- the pre-crisis period (July 1999 to November 2007), the crisis period (December 2007 to May 2009), and the post-crisis period (June 2009 to March 2017). Following modified dual-beta market model is estimated:

$$R_{Pt}-R_{Ft}= \alpha_0+ \alpha_1 D_1+\alpha_2 D_2+\beta_0 (R_{Mt}-R_{Ft})+ \beta_1 D_1 (R_{Mt}-R_{Ft})+\beta_2 D_2 (R_{Mt}-R_{Ft})+\varepsilon_t (4)$$

Where equals 1 for crisis months and 0 otherwise and equals 1 for Post-crisis months and 0 otherwise. α_0, $\alpha_0 + \alpha_1$, $\alpha_0 + \alpha_2$ represents excess return and β_0, $\beta_0 + \beta_1$, $\beta_0 + \beta_2$ represents beta coefficients for pre-crisis period, crisis and post-crisis periods respectively.

4. Empirical Analysis and Results

Table 1 shows the mean and standard deviations. For the full period, the mean returns of P1 are greater than P10 for all valuation proxies except for dividend yield. Strong value effect is confirmed using five alternative measures and average returns follow a declining trend almost monotonically from P1 to P10. However, Dividend yield sorted portfolios exhibit value discount as mean returns of P10 is higher than P1. This could be attributed to the low dividend yields of Indian companies. Value stocks provide returns that are almost double the returns on growth stocks. Though the value premium is documented for five valuation proxy measures, S/P sorted portfolios registered the highest value premium in the full period. Portfolio-wise mean returns for all valuation proxies are positive and higher in the boom than in the recessionary period. During the boom, the average monthly returns are large for P1 vis-a-vis P10. The highest value premium is yielded by S/P based VMG portfolio in the boom and recession. Similar results have been obtained for bullish and bearish phases. The

NMIMS
NMIMS
Management Review
ISSN: 0971-1023
Volume XXIX
Issue-3 | July 2021

portfolio returns are positive and higher in the bullish phase than in the bearish phase wherein the returns are negative. Despite negative returns, a positive value premium is achieved by all proxies except P/B during the bear period. The mean returns for all portfolios were positive in pre-crisis which took a dip in the crisis and turned negative. During post-crisis, all portfolios have positive and higher mean returns than the crisis. The standard deviation for the full period exhibits a similar pattern to the mean returns with large values for value stock portfolios. The high D/P portfolios are revealing higher return variability. The standard deviation for all portfolios for other periods tells a similar story. The value stock portfolios have higher return variability than growth stock portfolios and exhibit the highest values during the crisis followed by pre-crisis and post-crisis. The value stocks portfolios outshined growth stocks portfolios and market portfolios during the entire 18-years study period. S/P based VMG portfolio has registered the highest alphas in the full period, in the boom and recession, in the bearish phase and post-crisis. P/B based VMG portfolio has yielded the highest abnormal returns in the bullish market, pre-crisis period and crisis. Overall, the value stock portfolios for five valuation proxies have surpassed the growth stock portfolios and the market in each period.

NMIMS
Management Review
ISSN: 0971-1023
Volume XXIX
Issue-3 | July 2021

Table 1: Mean and Standard Deviations (σ) of Monthly Returns (%) for Portfolios

Portfolio	Full Period		Boom		Recession		Bull		Bear		Pre-crisis		Crisis		Post-crisis	
	Mean	σ	Mean	Σ	Mean	σ	Mean	Σ	Mean	σ	Mean	σ	Mean	σ	Mean	Σ
Panel A: Price to Book Ratio																
P1	2.95	11.81	5.31	11.95	0.02	10.94	10.13	10.57	-4.17	8.07	4.97	12.30	-0.02	18.42	1.35	8.93
P2	2.07	10.15	4.20	9.91	-0.58	9.81	8.39	8.58	-4.20	7.30	3.17	9.70	-0.73	18.11	1.42	8.13
P3	2.49	10.16	4.66	9.95	-0.21	9.76	9.14	8.00	-4.10	7.40	3.78	9.84	0.07	19.19	1.57	7.45
P4	1.94	9.24	3.77	8.94	-0.33	9.09	7.97	7.02	-4.03	7.03	2.81	8.87	0.04	17.77	1.38	6.82
P5	2.00	9.32	4.13	8.90	-0.65	9.14	8.04	7.31	-3.99	6.92	3.05	8.95	-0.36	18.59	1.32	6.47
P6	1.84	8.58	3.91	8.14	-0.74	8.42	7.69	6.19	-3.96	6.42	2.68	8.66	-0.76	15.78	1.43	6.04
P7	1.65	8.62	3.61	8.27	-0.78	8.43	7.59	6.28	-4.24	6.26	2.60	8.47	-1.02	17.70	1.15	5.36
P8	1.27	8.04	3.26	7.72	-1.22	7.73	6.76	5.88	-4.17	5.92	1.70	7.89	-0.31	16.51	1.10	5.17
P9	1.39	7.94	3.53	7.34	-1.28	7.85	6.75	5.33	-3.93	6.37	1.77	8.30	-1.23	15.01	1.47	4.92
P10	0.96	7.77	2.96	6.91	-1.52	8.06	6.08	5.35	-4.11	6.35	1.32	7.63	-1.43	16.38	1.03	4.66
VMG	1.99		2.34		1.55		4.05		-0.06		3.64		1.41		0.32	
Panel B: Price to Earnings Ratio																
P1	3.07	10.51	5.52	10.56	0.03	9.63	9.52	9.18	-3.32	7.37	4.38	10.44	0.52	18.93	2.15	7.80
P2	2.35	9.67	4.27	9.61	-0.04	9.19	8.59	7.92	-3.84	6.85	3.37	9.29	0.06	18.57	1.69	7.11
P3	2.35	8.79	4.43	8.54	-0.24	8.39	7.95	6.71	-3.21	6.86	3.28	8.69	-0.66	16.93	1.92	6.00
P4	2.05	8.82	4.17	8.50	-0.59	8.49	7.75	6.87	-3.60	6.64	2.90	8.64	-0.12	16.91	1.55	6.28
P5	2.02	8.81	3.86	8.37	-0.26	8.80	7.92	6.48	-3.82	6.66	3.11	8.57	-0.86	17.00	1.40	6.19
P6	1.53	8.26	3.65	7.72	-1.09	8.15	7.16	5.56	-4.03	6.54	1.94	8.01	-1.36	16.12	1.65	5.83
P7	1.48	8.15	3.36	7.48	-0.85	8.35	7.05	5.97	-4.04	5.98	1.96	8.16	-0.31	15.55	1.31	5.65
P8	1.34	7.86	3.23	7.39	-1.00	7.79	6.86	5.30	-4.12	5.93	1.82	7.91	-0.58	14.97	1.20	5.38

SVKM'S
NMIMS
Deemed-to-be UNIVERSITY

NMIMS
Management Review
ISSN: 0971-1023
Volume XXIX
Issue-3 | July 2021

NMIMS
Management Review
ISSN: 0971-1023
Volume XXIX
Issue-3 | July 2021

P9	4.94	0.89	15.66	-1.15	7.36	1.32	6.07	-4.22	5.00	6.11	7.90	-1.14	6.90	2.58	7.59	0.92
P10	6.50	0.28	20.13	-0.54	9.64	2.61	6.95	-5.55	7.32	8.24	9.75	-1.74	9.37	3.77	9.93	1.31
VMG		1.87		1.07		1.78		2.23		1.28		1.77		1.75		1.76
Panel C: Dividend Yield																
P1	6.72	1.18	15.77	-0.40	8.28	2.73	6.24	-3.71	6.99	7.33	8.39	-0.14	8.50	3.33	8.63	1.78
P2	6.61	1.50	15.70	-0.30	9.61	2.97	6.56	-3.99	7.30	8.14	8.71	-0.51	9.09	4.10	9.21	2.04
P3	6.03	1.16	15.23	-0.11	8.76	2.82	6.10	-3.83	6.64	7.56	7.99	-0.58	8.48	3.79	8.54	1.84
P4	6.25	1.53	15.02	-0.51	8.01	1.98	6.38	-3.80	5.94	6.99	7.78	-0.88	7.98	3.55	8.19	1.57
P5	5.75	1.45	15.83	-0.52	8.04	1.85	6.35	-3.97	5.79	6.96	8.09	-0.97	7.70	3.44	8.17	1.47
P6	5.89	1.47	17.73	-0.98	8.03	2.16	6.44	-3.97	6.51	7.21	8.37	-1.02	8.11	3.70	8.55	1.59
P7	5.96	1.16	19.80	-1.13	8.55	2.90	6.70	-4.31	7.06	7.95	9.05	-0.97	8.73	4.02	9.22	1.79
P8	5.86	1.05	18.91	-0.37	9.74	3.64	6.94	-4.13	7.55	8.51	9.68	-0.55	8.99	4.34	9.62	2.16
P9	6.62	1.40	20.00	-0.90	10.40	3.30	7.62	-4.51	8.10	8.79	9.80	-1.05	9.99	4.65	10.30	2.11
P10	7.50	1.41	19.66	-0.44	11.06	3.90	7.90	-4.76	8.28	9.69	10.71	-0.54	10.36	4.82	10.85	2.43
YVMG		-0.22		0.04		-1.17		1.05		-2.36		0.40		-1.49		-0.65
Panel D: Cash Flow Yield																
P1	8.33	1.56	17.98	-0.04	10.60	4.29	7.66	-3.85	9.03	9.35	10.05	0.33	10.75	4.64	10.66	2.72
P2	7.64	2.17	18.81	-0.35	10.41	3.66	7.73	-3.74	8.61	9.13	9.90	-0.37	10.16	5.11	10.41	2.67
P3	6.89	1.83	17.62	-0.42	9.36	3.41	6.98	-3.49	7.85	8.32	9.13	-0.40	9.17	4.64	9.49	2.39
P4	6.59	1.50	17.62	-1.26	9.75	3.16	6.96	-3.97	7.91	8.14	8.90	-0.66	9.58	4.24	9.60	2.05
P5	6.30	1.42	15.45	-0.87	9.49	3.11	6.95	-3.75	6.91	7.87	8.73	-0.50	8.78	4.06	9.05	2.03
P6	5.62	1.57	15.99	-0.18	8.12	2.32	6.30	-3.66	5.93	7.26	8.12	-0.76	7.69	3.81	8.20	1.77
P7	5.08	1.42	14.85	-0.39	8.23	2.41	6.16	-3.62	5.45	7.15	7.93	-0.52	7.44	3.56	7.93	1.74
P8	5.20	1.10	14.27	-1.00	7.61	1.09	5.35	-4.10	5.87	5.98	7.29	-1.24	7.29	2.65	7.55	0.92
P9	4.69	1.10	16.04	-0.34	7.95	1.41	6.05	-4.03	5.75	6.32	7.88	-1.17	7.32	2.96	7.85	1.12
P10	5.87	0.57	17.40	-1.39	8.68	1.68	6.49	-5.23	6.00	7.14	8.96	-1.46	8.17	2.85	8.79	0.93
VMG		0.99		1.35		2.61		1.38		2.21		1.79		1.79		1.79

Panel E: Sales to Price Ratio

P1	3.39	11.32	5.93	11.05	0.23	10.85	9.98	10.14	-3.14	8.22	4.62	12.02	-0.08	18.29	2.73	8.16
P2	2.48	10.52	4.90	10.27	-0.54	10.04	8.82	8.91	-3.81	7.90	3.26	10.46	0.06	19.11	2.10	7.84
P3	2.43	10.01	4.82	10.01	-0.55	9.18	8.71	8.22	-3.79	7.40	3.37	9.98	-0.46	18.45	1.97	7.22
P4	2.07	9.47	4.42	9.21	-0.84	8.96	8.19	7.53	-3.99	6.96	2.86	9.69	-0.67	17.08	1.75	6.64
P5	2.33	9.29	4.44	8.90	-0.28	9.11	8.39	6.99	-3.67	7.15	3.39	9.46	-0.54	17.72	1.75	6.04
P6	1.64	8.45	3.64	7.80	-0.85	8.57	7.19	6.25	-3.87	6.54	2.58	8.91	-1.48	14.74	1.22	5.65
P7	1.27	7.99	3.13	7.64	-1.04	7.80	6.63	5.62	-4.05	6.24	2.02	7.98	-0.99	15.34	0.90	5.41
P8	1.16	7.31	2.57	7.08	-0.60	7.21	5.97	5.57	-3.62	5.47	1.80	7.52	-0.30	14.12	0.75	4.60
P9	0.94	8.04	2.68	7.24	-1.21	8.44	6.20	5.91	-4.27	6.28	1.45	8.16	-0.98	16.70	0.77	4.53
P10	1.11	9.86	3.48	8.84	-1.84	10.26	8.21	6.76	-5.92	7.00	2.14	9.67	-0.50	19.54	0.31	6.67
VMG	2.28		2.45		2.08		1.77		2.78		2.48		0.42		2.42	

Panel F: Enterprise Value to PBDITA Ratio

P1	2.31	10.25	4.52	10.13	-0.43	9.72	8.82	8.29	-4.15	7.57	3.92	10.25	-0.41	17.93	1.10	7.62
P2	2.67	9.35	4.93	9.19	-0.13	8.78	8.72	7.43	-3.31	6.89	3.63	9.44	-0.15	16.78	2.18	6.76
P3	2.57	9.62	4.99	9.35	-0.43	9.11	8.86	7.50	-3.65	7.12	3.59	9.34	0.05	17.56	1.96	7.38
P4	2.11	9.51	4.24	9.46	-0.54	8.89	8.23	7.49	-3.95	7.13	3.20	9.29	-0.42	18.44	1.43	6.66
P5	1.80	8.83	3.73	8.47	-0.60	8.68	7.63	6.51	-3.98	6.81	2.61	8.49	-1.04	17.06	1.47	6.42
P6	1.69	9.18	3.70	8.90	-0.80	8.91	7.75	7.26	-4.32	6.57	2.20	8.60	0.01	19.16	1.46	6.35
P7	1.55	8.52	3.59	8.16	-0.98	8.27	7.32	6.33	-4.16	6.26	2.43	8.47	-0.90	15.99	1.08	6.01
P8	1.60	8.58	3.61	8.07	-0.91	8.55	7.48	6.36	-4.23	6.20	2.48	9.57	-0.85	14.23	1.12	5.25
P9	1.12	8.30	3.05	7.68	-1.27	8.43	6.57	6.09	-4.27	6.49	1.59	8.06	-1.53	17.32	1.13	5.25
P10	1.19	9.28	3.37	8.54	-1.52	9.45	7.72	6.49	-5.28	6.74	2.24	9.11	-0.56	19.27	0.39	5.70
VMG	1.12		1.15		1.08		1.10		1.14		1.68		0.15		0.71	
N	213		118		95		106		107		101		18		94	
Market	1.41	7.62	3.04	6.90	-0.61	7.97	7.12	4.51	-4.25	5.56	2.20	7.88	-0.92	14.38	1.00	4.83
Risk free rate	0.58	0.14	0.54	0.16	0.62	0.11	0.55	0.15	0.60	0.14	0.55	0.13	0.56	0.15	0.61	0.14

SVKM'S
NMIMS
Deemed to be UNIVERSITY

NMIMS
Management Review
ISSN: 0971-1023
Volume XXIX
Issue-3 | July 2021

Alphas over different periods using both single beta model and dual-beta market model as explained in equations (1) to (4) are reported for different valuation measures in Table 2.The Standard CAPM results show value portfolios have a higher alpha estimate than growth portfolios. The modified dual-beta market models are employed to estimate alphas for the economic cycles of boom and recession, bull and bear market and global financial crisis.

4.1 Price to Book Value (Panel A of Table 2)

P1 has an alpha of 1.9% whereas P10 has an alpha of0.10%. The value portfolios have higher alphas than growth portfolios in the boom. Value firms perform significantly better than growth firms in the boom than in the recessionary period. The alphas are marginally higher in the bull period than the bear period but no portfolio has significant differential returns ($\alpha_{bull-bear}$). Throughout pre-crisis, P1was yielding significant alphas of 3.2% whereas P10 produced -0.10% returns. Further, VMG generated a significant alpha of 3.3%. The alphas reduced considerably once the crisis hit. For the crisis, P1 (P10) has an alpha of 1.8% (0.2%). The VMG produced significant alphas of 1.5% for the crisis. Post-crisis, growth stocks outperformed value stocks. During the post-crisis period, alphas of value (growth) stock portfolios declined (increased) than their corresponding crisis values.P10 has a significant alpha of 0.7%throughoutpost-crisis as against 0.2% of crisis.

4.2 Price to Earnings Ratio (Panel B of Table 2)

P/E sorted P1has an alpha of 2.1% as against 0.3% of P10. The VMG is producing an alpha of 1.8% during the full period. The alpha of boom for all portfolios is significant. However, in the recessionary period, the alphas of P1, P2 and P5 are significant only. The VMG portfolio has an alpha of 1.6% during the boom and 1.5% in the recession. P1 has a significant alpha of 1.7% during the bearish phase whereas P10 yield negative alpha of 0.2%leading to a 1.9% monthly value premium. During the bullish phase, only P8 has a significant alpha of 1.7%. During pre-crisis, only value stock portfolios (P1 to P5) produced significant alphas. P1 is yielding significant alpha of 2.8% and the VMG is producing a 1.9% monthly value premium during pre-crisis. During the crisis period, the alphas of P1, P2 and P5 reduced considerably, however, the alphas of P7 and P10 increased significantly. But the differential alphas ($\alpha_{crisis-precrisis}$) were insignificant. The alphas are significant for all portfolios except P10 during post-crisis which has significant and negative differential alpha($\alpha_{postcrisis-precrisis}$). VMG reaped a 1.8% monthly value premium during post-crisis.

4.3 Dividend Yield (Panel C of Table 2)

Here, P10's alpha is 1.4% which is higher than P1's 0.9% alpha. During the boom period also, the alphas of growth stock portfolios are significantly higher than the alphas of value stock portfolios. The VMG strategy is producing negative and significant returns of 0.8%. This implies growth firms outperform value firms. During the recession, P1 is yielding significant returnsof0.9%.The differential alphas of recession and boom is significant and negative for P6, P8 and P9. These portfolios were adversely affected by recessionary conditions. Checking for market phases impact, moderate portfolios (P4, P5, P6, P7 and P8) produced significantly positive alphas during the bearish months. However, P2, P3 and P4 reaped significant alphas in the bullish months. During pre-crisis, P10 has an alpha of 2% as against 1.4% of P1. Compared to pre-crisis, the alphas are significantly lower (higher) for growth (value) stocks in the crisis. Although during post-crisis, alphas of all the portfolios are significant and lower than their corresponding pre-crisis alphas, the differential alpha is significant for P8 only.

4.4 Cash Flow to Price Ratio (Panel D of Table 2)

The alphas of value stock portfolios outperformed growth stock portfolios and reap the significant value premium of 1.7% in the full period. During the boom, all portfolios except P10 are yielding significant positive returns and P2 and P3 produced the highest alpha (1.9%). During the recession, only P1 produced significant alpha of 1.5%. The VMG portfolio reaped significant alpha of 1.7% (1.1%) during the recession (boom). Testing the impact of market conditions, P2 has an alpha of 1.6% during the bearish phase. The VMG portfolio has a significant alpha of 1.4% during the bearish phase. During the bullish phase, three portfolios (P3,P6 and P7) yielded significant alphas, the highest being registered by P3 (1.9%). In pre-crisis, P8, P9 and P10 performed poorly and produced insignificant and negative returns as against the significant returns of other portfolios. The value premium registered in pre-crisis for VMG is 2.6% per month. During the crisis, five portfolios yielded significant positive alphas and P2 has the highest alpha of 1.5%. The differential return ($\alpha_{crisis-precrisis}$) was significantly higher for P9 only. All portfolios except P10 produced significant returns post the crisis, the highest returns of 1.6% were produced by P2. The VMG portfolio has an alpha of 0.8%. In the post-crisis period, the differential return ($\alpha_{postcrisis-precrisis}$) was significantly lower (higher) for P1 (P8 and P9).

4.5 Sales to Price Ratio (Panel E of Table 2)

P1 has an alpha of 2.4% whereas P10 has an alpha of 0.10%. The alphas of most portfolios are significantly higher in the boom. During recessionary conditions, the returns remained significant for P1 and P5only.The VMG reaped a value premium of 1.8% during the recession. When the market conditions are accounted for, the alphas of value stock portfolios are significant during the bearish phase. The alphas are significantly higher in the bull period for P4 and P5. In pre-crisis, P1 has an alpha of 2.9% against 0.3%. The returns are significant for the first six portfolios (P1 to P6).

SVKM'S
NMIMS
Deemed to be UNIVERSITY

NMIMS
Management Review
ISSN: 0971-1023
Volume XXIX
Issue-3 | July 2021

The differential alpha ($\alpha_{\text{crisis-precrisis}}$) of the VMG portfolio is significant and negative suggesting returns on VMG reduced considerably during the crisis. The returns on all value stock portfolios remained significant during the crisis. P8 and P10 registered significant alphas in the crisis. The performance of returns improved post the crisis.

4.6 Enterprise Value to PBDITA Ratio (Panel F of Table 2)

During the full period, P1 has 1.3% alpha whereas P10 has an alpha of 0.2% leading to a 1.1% value premium. All the portfolios reaped significant returns and positive value premium during the boom. During the recession, P2 yielded significant returns only. The positive and significant alphas are present for P2, P3, P5 and P9during the bearish phase suggesting abnormal returns are greater for value stock portfolios than growth stock portfolios. Surprisingly, during the bullish period, only P3 and P7 registered significant alphas, wherein returns on P3 are greater than P7. During pre-crisis, P1 has an alpha of 2.3 % against 0.5% of P10. Compared to pre-crisis, the alphas are lower (higher) for value (growth) stock portfolios in the crisis period. However, the alphas are significant for P2, P3 and P10 only. During post-crisis, alphas of value (growth) stock portfolios are significant and lower (higher) than their corresponding pre-crisis alphas. The differential alpha is significant and lower for P1.

NMIMS
Management Review
ISSN: 0971-1023
Volume XXIX
Issue-3 | July 2021

Table 2: Alphas for Value Based Portfolios for Different Periods

Portfolio	Full Period		Economic Cycle			Bull-Bear			Global Financial Crisis				
	α_{full}	β_{full}	α_{boom}	$\alpha_{recession-boom}$	$\alpha_{recession}$	α_{bear}	$\alpha_{bull-bear}$	α_{bull}	$\alpha_{precrisis}$	$\alpha_{crisis-precrisis}$	α_{crisis}	$\alpha_{postcrisis-precrisis}$	$\alpha_{postcrisis}$
Panel A: Price to Book Ratio													
P1	0.019***	1.21***	0.018**	-0.005	0.012	0.008	0.003	0.011	0.032***	-0.014	0.018.	-0.024**	0.007
P2	0.011**	1.089***	0.012*	-0.006	0.006	0.005	-0.001	0.004	0.017*	-0.006	0.01	-0.008	0.008.
P3	0.015***	1.137***	0.015***	-0.005	0.01.	0.01.	0.003	0.013	0.021***	-0.002	0.019.	-0.011	0.01**
P4	0.01**	1.038***	0.009**	-0.001	0.008	0.009.	0.003	0.012	0.013*	0.004	0.018**	-0.004	0.008**
P5	0.011***	1.064***	0.012***	-0.007	0.005	0.01*	-0.005	0.005	0.015**	0	0.014**	-0.007	0.008**
P6	0.01***	0.993***	0.013***	-0.009	0.003	0.007	0.007	0.015*	0.011*	-0.003	0.008	-0.001	0.009**
P7	0.007**	1.034***	0.008**	-0.004	0.004	0.006.	0	0.005	0.01*	-0.002	0.007	-0.002	0.007**
P8	0.004*	0.947***	0.007*	-0.008.	0.002	0.002	0.001	0.004	0.002	0.01	0.013*	0.004	0.007**
P9	0.006**	0.94***	0.011***	-0.013**	-0.001	0.009**	0.002	0.012*	0.002	0	0.002	0.008.	0.011***
P10	0.001	0.94***	0.006*	-0.01*	-0.003	0.007.	-0.012	-0.004	-0.001	0.003	0.002	0.008.	0.007*
VMG	0.017**	0.27***	0.011.	0.004	0.016.	0	0.015	0.016	0.033***	-0.017	0.015.	-0.033**	0
Panel B: Price to Earnings Ratio													
P1	0.021***	1.131***	0.022***	-0.01	0.011.	0.017**	-0.006	0.01	0.028***	-0.004	0.024**	-0.012	0.016**
P2	0.014***	1.058***	0.013**	-0.002	0.011.	0.006	0.003	0.009	0.019**	0	0.018.	-0.007	0.011**
P3	0.015***	0.999***	0.017***	-0.008	0.008	0.018***	-0.004	0.013	0.018**	-0.008	0.01	-0.003	0.014***
P4	0.012***	0.995***	0.015***	-0.01	0.005	0.01*	-0.002	0.007	0.014**	0	0.015*	-0.003	0.011**
P5	0.011***	1.02***	0.011***	-0.002	0.008.	0.01*	0.001	0.012	0.016***	-0.008	0.008.	-0.007	0.009***
P6	0.007**	0.986***	0.011**	-0.01*	0	0.009*	0	0.009	0.004	-0.002	0.002	0.007	0.012***
P7	0.006**	0.946***	0.009***	-0.006	0.002	0.002	0.004	0.007	0.005	0.006	0.012*	0.003	0.008***
P8	0.005*	0.927***	0.008**	-0.007	0	0.004	0.012*	0.017**	0.004	0.005	0.009	0.003	0.008***
P9	0.001	0.916***	0.002	-0.002	0	0.006.	0	0.006	0	0.004	0.004	0.005	0.005*

NMIMS
Management Review
ISSN: 0971-1023
Volume XXIX
Issue-3 | July 2021

P10	0.003	1.188***	0.006.	-0.01.	-0.003	-0.002	0.001	-0.001	0.008	0.006	0.014.	-0.01.	-0.001
VMG	0.018***	-0.057	0.016**	0	0.015*	0.019***	-0.008	0.011	0.019**	-0.01	0.009	-0.001	0.018***

Panel C: Dividend Yield

P1	0.009**	0.948***	0.007*	0.001	0.009.	0.005	0.002	0.007	0.014**	-0.002	0.011	-0.007	0.007*
P2	0.011***	1.027***	0.013**	-0.006	0.006	0.006	0.007	0.013.	0.013*	-0.001	0.012	-0.003	0.01**
P3	0.01**	0.968***	0.011**	-0.006	0.004	0.005	0.006	0.011.	0.013*	0	0.014**	-0.006	0.007*
P4	0.007**	0.944***	0.009**	-0.008	0.001	0.009*	0.002	0.011.	0.006	0.003	0.009.	0.004	0.01**
P5	0.006**	0.967***	0.009**	-0.007	0.001	0.008*	-0.001	0.006	0.004	0.006	0.01*	0.006	0.01***
P6	0.007*	0.998***	0.01**	-0.009.	0	0.009*	-0.005	0.003	0.007	0	0.007	0.002	0.01***
P7	0.008***	1.085***	0.011***	-0.008.	0.002	0.007.	-0.005	0.001	0.013***	-0.005	0.008	-0.006	0.007**
P8	0.012***	1.11***	0.014***	-0.006	0.007	0.01*	-0.003	0.007	0.019***	-0.004	0.015*	-0.013*	0.006*
P9	0.011***	1.159***	0.014***	-0.012.	0.002	0.008	0	0.007	0.016**	-0.005	0.01	-0.007	0.009**
P10	0.014***	1.233***	0.016**	-0.007	0.009	0.007	0.005	0.012	0.02**	-0.005	0.015.	-0.011	0.008*
YVMG	-0.004	-0.285***	-0.008*	0.009	0	-0.002	-0.002	-0.004	-0.006	0.002	-0.003	0.004	-0.001

Panel D: Cash Flow Yield

P1	0.017***	1.136***	0.014**	0.001	0.015*	0.01	0	0.011	0.026***	-0.009	0.017	-0.016*	0.009*
P2	0.017***	1.134***	0.019***	-0.011	0.008	0.016*	-0.003	0.012	0.02**	-0.005	0.015**	-0.004	0.016***
P3	0.015***	1.005***	0.019***	-0.012	0.006	0.012*	0.007	0.019.	0.02**	-0.007	0.013*	-0.007	0.013***
P4	0.011**	1.062***	0.012**	-0.007	0.004	0.008.	-0.003	0.005	0.016**	-0.011	0.004	-0.005	0.01**
P5	0.011***	1.017***	0.013**	-0.007	0.006	0.011*	0	0.012	0.015**	-0.008	0.006	-0.006	0.009***
P6	0.009***	0.946***	0.013***	-0.01*	0.003	0.01**	0.004	0.015.	0.009*	0.004	0.014**	0.002	0.011***
P7	0.009***	0.922***	0.012***	-0.006	0.005	0.01**	0.008	0.018**	0.009*	0.001	0.01*	0	0.01***
P8	0.002	0.85***	0.003	-0.006	-0.003	-0.001	0.009	0.007	-0.001	0.005	0.004	0.008.	0.007***
P9	0.003	0.935***	0.004*	-0.005	0	0.007*	-0.007	0	0	0.013*	0.012*	0.007*	0.007***
P10	0	1.056***	0.002	-0.003	-0.001	-0.003	0.006	0.002	0	0.002	0.003	0	0.001
VMG	0.017***	0.08	0.011*	0.005	0.017*	0.014.	-0.005	0.008	0.026**	-0.012	0.013	-0.017.	0.008.

SVKM's
NMIMS
Deemed to be UNIVERSITY

NMIMS
Management Review
ISSN: 0971-1023
Volume XXIX
Issue-3 | July 2021

Panel E: Sales to Price Ratio

P1	0.024***	1.133***	0.028***	-0.013	0.014.	0.019*	0	0.019	0.029**	-0.012	0.017.	-0.007	0.022***
P2	0.015***	1.108***	0.018***	-0.012	0.006	0.014*	-0.001	0.012	0.017*	0.002	0.019.	-0.001	0.015**
P3	0.015***	1.091***	0.017***	-0.011	0.005	0.012*	-0.001	0.011	0.018**	-0.004	0.013.	-0.003	0.014***
P4	0.011***	1.051***	0.015***	-0.012.	0.002	0.01*	0.004	0.015.	0.013*	-0.002	0.01.	0	0.012***
P5	0.014***	1.032***	0.017***	-0.008	0.008.	0.011.	0.006	0.017.	0.018**	-0.006	0.012*	-0.005	0.013***
P6	0.008**	0.981***	0.01***	-0.007	0.002	0.01*	-0.002	0.007	0.01*	-0.01	0	-0.002	0.008**
P7	0.004*	0.94***	0.006*	-0.006	0	0.006	0	0.005	0.005	0	0.005	0	0.005*
P8	0.004*	0.841***	0.003	0	0.003	0.003	-0.001	0.001	0.005	0.005	0.011*	-0.001	0.004*
P9	0.001	0.927***	0.002	-0.004	-0.001	0.005	0	0.004	0	0.006	0.006	0.003	0.004*
P10	0.001	1.195***	0.006.	-0.009.	-0.003	-0.004	0.01	0.005	0.003	0.011	0.014*	-0.004	-0.001
VMG	0.023***	-0.061	0.022***	-0.004	0.018.	0.024**	-0.009	0.014	0.026**	-0.024*	0.002	-0.002	0.023***

Panel F: Enterprise Value to PBDITA Ratio

P1	0.013**	1.116***	0.015**	-0.007	0.008	0.007	0.001	0.009	0.023**	-0.009	0.013	-0.017*	0.005
P2	0.018***	1.041***	0.021***	-0.011	0.01*	0.013*	0	0.012	0.02***	-0.005	0.015*	-0.003	0.017***
P3	0.016***	1.071***	0.02***	-0.013.	0.007	0.014**	0.006	0.021*	0.02***	-0.002	0.017*	-0.006	0.014**
P4	0.012***	1.069***	0.012**	-0.006	0.006	0.009	-0.003	0.005	0.017**	-0.002	0.014	-0.007	0.009**
P5	0.009**	1.011***	0.01**	-0.004	0.005	0.01*	0.002	0.012	0.011*	-0.005	0.006	-0.001	0.01**
P6	0.008*	1.042***	0.008*	-0.004	0.003	0.003	0	0.003	0.007	0.011	0.018	0.002	0.009***
P7	0.007**	0.982***	0.009**	-0.008	0.001	0.004	0.005	0.01	0.01*	-0.003	0.007	-0.003	0.006**
P8	0.007**	1.001***	0.01***	-0.007	0.002	0.005	0.006	0.012*	0.007.	-0.001	0.005	0	0.007**
P9	0.003	0.976***	0.004.	-0.006	-0.001	0.007.	-0.005	0.001	0.001	0	0.002	0.005	0.007**
P10	0.002	1.13***	0.005.	-0.006	-0.001	0	0	-0.001	0.005	0.008	0.013.	-0.005	0
VMG	0.011*	-0.014	0.01.	0	0.009	0.008	0.001	0.01	0.018*	-0.018	0	-0.012	0.005

'.', '*', '**', and '***' indicate significance at 10%, 5%, 1% and 0.1% respectively.

SVKM'S
NMIMS
Deemed to be UNIVERSITY

NMIMS
Management Review
ISSN: 0971-1023
Volume XXIX
Issue-3 | July 2021

5. Discussion and Conclusion

The paper analysed the impact of different business cycles, stock market phases, and crisis on the value premium in the Indian stock market. Looking at the α_{boom} results, barring a few growth stock portfolios, the alphas are positive and significant for all portfolios. In sharp contrast, the alphas are rarely significant and positive during the recession and decline drastically in recessionary conditions. Thus, it can be inferred that irrespective of boom or recession; value portfolios have an edge over growth portfolios in generating positive excess returns.

Moving on to the impact of bull and bear market phases on the value premium, except for a few growth stock portfolios, the alphas are generally positive in both bull and bear periods. Similar to the economic condition, the alpha values fall in the bearish phase too, as P10 generates negative returns when sorted using P/E, CF/P, and S/P. Interestingly, the value stock portfolios have managed to produce significant excess returns in the bearish phase suggesting value stock portfolios are a good investment when the markets are down.

The alphas are significantly positive in pre-crisis for all value stock portfolios of all valuation proxies. During the crisis, alphas were significant for a few portfolios only. In post-crisis, most of the portfolios are producing significant alphas. While the value premium is significant for five valuation measures during pre-crisis, it remained positive and significant for only P/B during the crisis/E, CF/P and S/P based value premium were significant during post-crisis. This implies that investors put faith in the value stocks in times of adversity

Overall, this paper discussed whether value stock portfolios can outperform the growth stock portfolios during different business economic and market conditions- domestic and international. Consistent with previous studies (Lakonishok, Shleifer and Vishny, 1994; Santos and Montezano, 2011; Hsieh, 2015), the empirical results show that value stock portfolios outperformed growth stock portfolios in each state of the Indian economy analysed and even managed to produce higher returns in adverse conditions- recession, bear period, or crisis. The alphas of value stock portfolios were found to be higher than their growth counterparts. The study also found that the returns for value stocks and growth stocks are not significantly different during expansionary and recessionary phases of the Indian economic cycle (Beckers and Thomas, 2010).

The paper is not free from certain limitations. Firstly, due to the non-availability of data in the public domain, the period before 1999 could not be considered. Secondly, the study has used data of BSE-500 companies only; however, future researchers can include both NSE and BSE companies. Moreover, the study did not control for firm size while forming portfolios; therefore, value-weighted portfolios can be formed in the future.

To conclude, Value Investing is a winning strategy when the markets are facing adverse conditions. The investor should keep in mind that stocks become riskier as their price rises and less risky as their prices fall. A value investor usually dreads a recessionary and crisis-prone market and welcomes a boom and non-crisis market. However, these adverse conditions are good news for value investors. Because of the overall decline in stock prices, these periods are a considerably safer time to build wealth. As an old saying goes, *markets go up through the staircase and come down on an elevator*. Unnerving that it is, value investing helps investors navigate through this falling market. The recession and bearish market phase offer a good opportunity for value investors to buy more of the stocks since the stock prices for value stocks are cheaper. Value stocks can act as a hedge in these uncertain times. This has constructive implications for investors and portfolio managers as they can follow the value investment strategy that may provide extra-normal returns while managing their portfolios.

References

Ang, A. and Bekaert, G. (2007) 'Stock return predictability: Is it there?', *Review of Financial Studies*, 20(3), pp. 651–707. doi: 10.1093/rfs/hhl021.

Arshanapalli, B. G. and Nelson, W. B. (2007) 'Small Cap and Value Investing Offer both High Returns and a Hedge', *The Journal of Wealth Management*, 9(4), pp. 44–50. doi: 10.3905/jwm.2007.674806.

Artmann, S., Finter, P. and Kempf, A. (2012) 'Determinants of Expected Stock Returns: Large Sample Evidence from the German Market', *Journal of Business Finance and Accounting*, 39(5–6), pp. 758–784. doi: 10.1111/j.1468-5957.2012.02286.x.

Athanassakos, G. (2009) 'Value versus growth stock returns and the value premium: The Canadian experience 1985-2005', *Canadian Journal of Administrative Sciences*, 26(2), pp. 109–121. doi: 10.1002/cjas.93.

Athanassakos, G. (2011) 'The Performance, Pervasiveness and Determinants of Value Premium in Different US Exchanges: 1985-2006', *The Journal of Investment Management*, 9, pp. 33–73.

Ball, R. (1978) 'Anomalies in relationships between securities' yields and yield-surrogates', *Journal of Financial Economics*, 6(2–3), pp. 103–126. doi: 10.1016/0304-405X(78)90026-0.

Banerjee, A., De, A. and Bandyopadhyay, G. (2018) 'Momentum effect, value effect, risk premium and predictability of stock returns – A study on Indian market', *Asian Economic and Financial Review*. Asian Economic and Social Society, 8(5), pp. 669–681. doi: 10.18488/journal.aefr.2018.85.669.681.

Barbee, W. C., Mukherji, S. and Raines, G. A. (1996) 'Do sales-price and debt-equity explain stock returns better than book-market and firm size?', *Financial Analysts Journal*, 52(2), pp. 56–60. doi: 10.2469/faj.v52.n2.1980.

Basu, S. (1977) 'Investment Performance of Common Stocks in Relation to Their Price-

NMIMS

NMIMS
Management Review
ISSN: 0971-1023
Volume XXIX
Issue-3 | July 2021

Earning Ratio: A Test of the Efficient Market Hypothesis', *The Journal of Business*, pp. 663–682. doi: 10.1111/j.1540-6261.1977.tb01979.x.

Beckers, S. and Thomas, J. A. (2010) 'On the persistence of style returns', *Journal of Portfolio Management*, 37(1), pp. 15–30. doi: 10.4161/psb.26964.

Bekaert, G., Harvey, C. R. and Lundblad, C. (2007) 'Liquidity and Expected Returns : Lessons from', *The Review of Financial Studies*, 20(5), pp. 1784–1831. doi: 10.1093/rfs/hhm030.

Bhardwaj, R. K. and Brooks, L. R. D. (1993) 'Dual Betas From Bull and Bear Markets: Reversal of the Size Effect', *Journal of Financial Research*, 16(4), pp. 269–283. doi: 10.1111/j.1475-6803.1993.tb00147.x.

Bird, R. and Casavecchia, L. (2007) 'Value enhancement using momentum indicators: the European experience', *International Journal of Managerial Finance*, 3(3), pp. 229–262. doi: 10.1108/17439130710756907.

Brown, S. *et al.* (2008) 'The returns to value and momentum in Asian Markets', *Emerging Markets Review*, 9(2), pp. 79–88. doi: 10.1016/j.ememar.2008.02.001.

Cakici, N., Tang, Y. and Yan, A. (2016) 'Do the size, value, and momentum factors drive stock returns in emerging markets?', *Journal of International Money and Finance*. Elsevier Ltd, 69, pp. 179–204. doi: 10.1016/j.jimonfin.2016.06.001.

Capaul, C., Rowley, I. and Sharpe, W. F. (1993) 'International Value and Growth Stock Returns', *Financial Analysts Journal*, 49(1), pp. 27–36. doi: 10.2469/faj.v49.n1.27.

Chan, L. K. C. C. and Lakonishok, J. (2004) 'Value and growth investing: Review and update', *Financial Analysts Journal*, 60(1), pp. 71–86. doi: 10.2469/faj.v60.n1.2593.

Chan, L. K. C., Hamao, Y. and Lakonishok, J. (1991) 'Fundamentals and Stock Returns in Japan', *Journal of Finance*, 46(5), p. 1739. doi: 10.2307/2328571.

Cheh, J. J., Kim, D. and Zheng, G. (2008) 'Investing in Growth Stocks vs. Value Stocks', *The Journal of Investing*, 17(2), pp. 75–92. doi: 10.3905/joi.2008.707220.

Chen, L., Petkova, R. and Zhang, L. (2008) 'The expected value premium', *Journal of Financial Economics*, 87(2), pp. 269–280. doi: 10.1016/j.jfineco.2007.04.001.

Damodaran, A. (2012) 'Growth Investing : Betting on the future ? Aswath Damodaran Stern School of Business New York University Email : adamodar@stern.nyu.edu July 2012 Growth Investing : Betting on the future ?', (July), pp. 1–52.

Dhatt, M. S., Kim, Y. H. and Mukherji, S. (2004) 'Can Composite Value Measures Enhance Portfolio Performance?', *The Journal of Investing*, 13(4), pp. 42–48. doi: 10.3905/joi.2004.450755.

Dissanaike, G. and Lim, K. (2007) 'The Sophisticated and the Simple : the profitability of contrarian strategies The Sophisticated and the Simple : the profitability of contrarian strategies', 16(2), pp. 229–255. doi: 10.1111/j.1468-036X.2008.00466.x.

Ebrahim, M. S. Girma, S., Shah, M.E. and Williams, J. (2014) 'Rationalizing the value premium in emerging markets', *Journal of International Financial Markets, Institutions and Money*. Elsevier B.V., 29(1), pp. 51–70. doi: 10.1016/j.intfin.2013.11.005.

NMIMS
Management Review
ISSN: 0971-1023
Volume XXIX
Issue-3 | July 2021

Fama, E. F. and French, K. R. (1993) 'Common risk factors in the returns on stocks and bonds', *Journal of Financial Economics*, 33(1), pp. 3–56. doi: 10.1016/0304-405X(93)90023-5.

Fama, E. F. and French, K. R. (1996) 'Mulitfactor Explanations of Asset Pricing Anomalies', *Journal of Finance*, 51(1), pp. 55–84.

Fama, E. F. and French, K. R. (1998) 'Value Versus Growth : the International Evidence', *Journal of Finance*, 53(6), pp. 1975–1999. doi: 10.1111/0022-1082.00080.

Fama, E. F. and French, K. R. (2006) 'Profitability, investment and average returns', *Journal of Financial Economics*, 82(3), pp. 491–518. doi: 10.1016/j.jfineco.2005.09.009.

Fama, E. F. and French, K. R. (2007a) 'Migration', *Financial Analysts Journal*, 63(3), pp. 48–58. doi: 10.2469/faj.v63.n3.4690.

Fama, E. F. and French, K. R. (2007b) 'The anatomy of value and growth stock returns', *Financial Analysts Journal*, 63(6), pp. 44–54. doi: 10.2469/faj.v63.n6.4926.

Fama, E. F. and French, K. R. (2008) 'Average returns, B/M, and share issues', *Journal of Finance*, 63(6), pp. 2971–2995. doi: 10.1111/j.1540-6261.2008.01418.x.

Fama, E. F. and French, K. R. (2012) 'Size, value, and momentum in international stock returns', *Journal of Financial Economics*. Elsevier, 105(3), pp. 457–472. doi: 10.1016/j.jfineco.2012.05.011.

Fama, E. and French, K. (1992) 'The cross-section of expected stock returns', *JoF*, pp. 427–466. doi: 10.2307/2329112.

Foye, J. (2016) 'A new perspective on the size, value, and momentum effects Broad sample evidence from Europe', *Review of Accounting and Finance*, 15(2), pp. 222–251. doi: 10.1108/RAF-05-2015-0065.

Garcia, M.T.M and Oliveira, R. A. . (2018) 'Article information : Value versus growth in PIIGS stock markets', *Journal of Economic Studies*, 45(5), pp. 956–978.

Gharghori, P., Stryjkowski, S. and Veeraraghavan, M. (2013) 'Value versus growth: Australian evidence', *Accounting and Finance*, 53(2), pp. 393–417. doi: 10.1111/j.1467-629X.2012.00474.x.

Graham, B. and Dodd, D. (1934) *Security Analysis, Analysis*. doi: 10.1036/0071592539.

Gray, W. R. and Vogel, J. (2012) 'Analyzing valuation measures: A performance horse race over the past 40 years', *Journal of Portfolio Management*, 39(1), pp. 112–121. doi: 10.3905/jpm.2012.39.1.112.

Gregory, A., Harris, R. D. F. and Michou, M. (2001) 'An Analysis of Contrarian Strategies in the UK.', *Journal of Business Finance and Accounting*, 28((9) & (10),), pp. 1193–1228.

van der Hart, J., de Zwart, G. and van Dijk, D. (2005) 'The success of stock selection strategies in emerging markets: Is it risk or behavioral bias?', *Emerging Markets Review*, 6(3), pp. 238–262. doi: 10.1016/j.ememar.2005.05.002.

Hou, K., Karolyi, G. A. and Kho, B. C. (2011) 'What factors drive global stock returns?', *Review of Financial Studies*, 24(8), pp. 2527–2574. doi: 10.1093/rfs/hhr013.

NMIMS

**NMIMS
Management Review**
ISSN: 0971-1023
Volume XXIX
Issue-3 | July 2021

Hsieh, H. H. (2015) 'Empirical investigation of the value effect in the large and small cap segments of the JSE: Evidence from the South African stock market', *Investment Management and Financial Innovations*, 12(4), pp. 16–22.

Hu, G. X. *et al.* (2018) 'Fama–French in China: Size and Value Factors in Chinese Stock Returns', *International Review of Finance*, (201506135009), pp. 1–11. doi: 10.1111/ir.

Huang, I. H. (2011) 'The cyclical behavior of the risk of value strategy: Evidence from Taiwan', *Pacific Basin Finance Journal*. Elsevier B.V., 19(4), pp. 404–419. doi: 10.1016/j.pacfin.2011.03.002.

Jensen, M. C. (1968) 'THE PERFORMANCE OF MUTUAL FUNDS IN THE PERIOD 1945-1964', *The Journal of Finance*, 23(2). doi: 10.1111/j.1540-6261.1968.tb00815.x.

Keim, D. B. (1985) 'Dividend yields and stock returns: Implications of abnormal January returns', *Journal of Financial Economics*, 14(3), pp. 473–489. doi: 10.1016/0304-405X(85)90009-1.

Kim, M. K. and Burnie, D. A. (2002) 'The firm size effect and the economic cycle', *Journal of Financial Research*, 25(1), pp. 111–124. doi: 10.1111/1475-6803.00007.

Lakonishok, J., Shleifer, A. and Vishny, R. W. (1994) 'Contrarian Investment, Extrapolation, and Risk', *The Journal of Finance*, 49(5), pp. 1541–1578. doi: 10.1111/j.1540-6261.1994.tb04772.x.

Leivo, T. and Patari, E. (2009) 'The Impact of Holding Period Length on Value Portfolio Performance in the Finnish Stock Markets', *Journal of Money, Investment and Banking*, 8(8), pp. 71–86.

Leledakis, G. and Davidson, I. (2001) 'Are Two Factors Enough? The U.K. Evidence', *Financial Analysts Journal*, 57(6), pp. 96–105. doi: 10.2469/faj.v57.n6.2496.

Li, X., Brooks, C. and Miffre, J. (2011) 'The Value Premium and Time-Varying Volatility', *SSRN Electronic Journal*, 33(0), pp. 1252–1272. doi: 10.2139/ssrn.983905.

Lintner, J. (1965) 'The Valuation of Risk Assets and the Selection of Risky Investments in Stock Portfolios and Capital Budgets', *The Review of Economics and Statistics*, 47(1). doi: 10.2307/1924119.

Loughran, T. and Wellman, J. W. (2011) 'New evidence on the relation between the enterprise multiple and average stock returns', *Journal of Financial and Quantitative Analysis*, 46(6), pp. 1629–1650. doi: 10.1017/S0022109011000445.

Pätäri, E. J., Karell, V. and Luukka, P. (2016) 'Can size-, industry-, and leverage-adjustment of valuation ratios benefit the value investor?', *International Journal of Business Innovation and Research*, 11(1), pp. 76–109.

Pätäri, E. and Leivo, T. (2017) 'a Closer Look At Value Premium: Literature Review and Synthesis', *Journal of Economic Surveys*, 31(1), pp. 79–168. doi: 10.1111/joes.12133.

Penman, S. and Reggiani, F. (2013) 'Returns to buying earnings and book value: Accounting for growth and risk', *Review of Accounting Studies*, 18(4), pp. 1021–1049. doi: 10.1007/s11142-013-9226-y.

Reddy, K., Qamar, M. A. J. and Rao, M. (2019) 'Return reversal effect in Shanghai A share

NMIMS
Management Review
ISSN: 0971-1023
Volume XXIX
Issue-3 | July 2021

market', *Managerial Finance*, 45(6), pp. 698–715. doi: 10.1108/MF-04-2018-0140.

Rosenberg, B., Reid, K. and Lanstein, R. (1985) 'Persuasive evidence of market inefficiency', *Journal of Portfolio Management*, 11(3), pp. 9–16. doi: 10.3905/jpm.1985.409007.

Rouwenhorst, K. G. (1999) 'Local return factors and turnover in emerging stock markets', *Journal of Finance*, 54(4), pp. 1439–1464. doi: 10.1111/0022-1082.00151.

Rutledge, R. W., Zhang, Z. and Karim, K. (2008) 'Is there a size effect in the pricing of stocks in the chinese stock markets?: The case of bull versus bear markets', *Asia-Pacific Financial Markets*, 15(2), pp. 117–133. doi: 10.1007/s10690-008-9074-0.

Santos, L. da R. and Montezano, R. M. da S. (2011) 'Value and growth stocks in Brazil: risks and returns for one - and two-dimensional portfolios under different economic conditions', *Revista Contabilidade & Finanças*, 22(56), pp. 189–202. doi: 10.1590/s1519-70772011000200005.

Senchack, A. J. and Martin, J. D. (1987) 'The Relative Performance of the PSR and PER Investment Strategies', *Financial Analysts Journal*, 43(2). doi: 10.2469/faj.v43.n2.46.

Sharpe, W. F. (1964) 'Capital asset prices: A theroy of market equilibrium under conditions of risk', *The Journal of Finance*, 19(3), pp. 425–442. doi: 10.2307/2329297.

Sobti, N. (2018) 'Does Size, Value and Seasonal Effects Still Persist in Indian Equity Markets?', *Vision*, 22(1), pp. 11–21. doi: 10.1177/0972262917750230.

Switzer, L. N. (2010) 'The behaviour of small cap vs. large cap stocks in recessions and recoveries: Empirical evidence for the United States and Canada', *North American Journal of Economics and Finance*. Elsevier Inc., 21(3), pp. 332–346. doi: 10.1016/j.najef.2010.10.002.

Teh, K.-S. and Lau, W.-Y. (2017) 'The Dual-Beta Model: Evidence from the Malaysian Stock Market', *Indonesian Capital Market Review*, 9(1), pp. 39–52. doi: 10.21002/icmr.v9i1.6367.

Tripathi, V. and Aggarwal, P. (2018) 'Value effect in Indian stock market: An empirical analysis', *International Journal of Public Sector Performance Management*, 4(2). doi: 10.1504/IJPSPM.2018.090735.

Tripathi, V. and Aggarwal, P. (2020) 'Is value premium sector-specific? Evidence from India', *Managerial Finance*, 46(12), pp. 1605–1628. doi: 10.1108/MF-02-2020-0049.

Yen, J. Y., Sun, Q. and Yan, Y. (2004) 'Value versus growth stocks in Singapore', *Journal of Multinational Financial Management*, 14(1), pp. 19–34. doi: 10.1016/S1042-444X(03)00036-7.

Priti Aggarwal is senior research fellow at Department of Commerce, Delhi school of Economics, University of Delhi and can be reached at priti3789@gmail.com. Her ORCID id is 0000-0002-5898-030X.

Vanita Tripathi is Professor at Department of Commerce, Delhi school of Economics, University of Delhi and can be reached at vanitatripathi.dse@gmail.com

NMIMS

NMIMS Management Review
ISSN: 0971-1023
Volume XXIX
Issue-3 | July 2021

Effects of Demonetization, GST & Covid-19 Pandemic in the Adoption of Digitalization by Rural MSMEs in India

Received: 27 Mar 2021
Revised: 19 July 2021
Accepted: 4 Sept 2021

https://doi.org/10.53908/NMMR.290302

Shafique Ahmed • Samiran Sur

Abstract

Purpose: The turbulent times created by the recent uncertain events give only two solutions – either surrender or fight-out. It has been the story so far for the MSMEs in India. Three events that changed the business scenario include the implementation of demonetization & GST and the pandemic-related restrictions. Survival became the only viable factor for businesses. This study dwells deeper into these three events and their influence on the adoption of digitalization by MSMEs in rural India.

Methodology: Responses of the rural MSME owners were collected through a structured questionnaire containing multiple-choice questions on a 5-point Likert scale. To have better clarity, responses of 274 rural MSME owners were finally considered for the data analysis. For factor analysis of the data, the process of Principal Component Analysis (PCA) was adopted with the help of IBM SPSS 25.0. To find out the validity of the model, Structural Equation Modelling (SEM) was performed by using IBM AMOS 21.0.

Findings: It is found that the pandemic effect has the strongest significance followed by the demonetization effect on MSME owners towards the adoption of digitalization for their business. GST was implemented within a year of demonetization, so its effect is found to be non-significant.

Practical Implications: The results of the study will help the government as well as IT solution providers to chalk out their strategies, products, or reforms taking into consideration the particular problems faced by MSMEs related to demonetization and pandemic closure. The outcome will also help in better implementation of the 'Vocal for Local' initiative.

Originality: The results of the proposed study indicate that during all the three major events, the importance of digitalization has been witnessed by the MSMEs. These uncertain times have prioritized the use of digitalization not only for their survival but also to match the consumers' demands during those periods. This study shows

NMIMS

NMIMS
Management Review
ISSN: 0971-1023
Volume XXIX
Issue-3 | July 2021

the importance of digitalization and will help the cup to reach the lip and both the economy and the MSME owners will be benefitted from it.

Keywords: *Demonetization, GST, Pandemic, Covid-19, Digitalization, Vocal for Local, MSME*

1. Introduction

The world is gripped in uncertain times. The current pandemic has thrown us back several years. Almost every country is facing a huge economic crisis and unemployment is reaching a record high. The current situation in India is not healthy for its economic development. The production, sales, and operation of almost every business are yet to come to their full strength. We are still uncertain whether the situation is coming into control or going away farther leaving its destructive trail behind. In India, one important sector that is badly affected is the MSME (Micro Small and Medium Enterprises). This sector is considered as the backbone of Indian economy. The contribution of MSMEs in manufacturing Gross Domestic Product (GDP) is around 6.11 percent and services GDP is 24.63 percent. It gives around 33.4 percent of India's manufacturing output. With a constant growth rate of over 10 percent, this sector employs around 120 Crores people (CII, 2020). The two biggest economic reforms in India, in the form of Demonetization (2016) and Goods and Services Tax - GST (2017) and the destructive Covid-19 pandemic (2020) have crippled this sector. Many units are either fully closed or working with reduced strength or operations. This sector is the biggest employment provider in India and is present in almost every corner of the country. The current devastation of the pandemic has forced the government to change the classification of MSMEs. With effect from July 2020, the classification of MSMEs is based on two factors – Investment and turnover. Micro enterprises are those with an investment of less than 1 crore and a turnover of less than 5 Crores while small enterprises come under the category with an investment of less than 10 Crores and a turnover of fewer than 50 Crores. Finally, Medium enterprises are those with an investment of fewer than 50 Crores and an annual turnover of less the 250 Crores (MSME, GOI, 2020). Coming days will justify whether the change in the classification of MSMEs is effective in its revival or not. The government has come up with another idea called Creation and Harmonious Application of Modern Process for Increasing the Output and National Strength (CHAMPION). It is a technology-driven single window system to help and promote MSMEs. It will take care of the financing aspect, raw materials procurement, labor needs and the different permissions related to the smooth functioning of the units. It will also create new opportunities in both manufacturing as well as services sectors (GOI, 2020).

We are in an era where digital innovation has become an integral part of our day–to-day life. Better and affordable electronic devices and affordable high-speed internet

NMIMS
Management Review
ISSN: 0971-1023
Volume XXIX
Issue-3 | July 2021

is fuelling the growth towards a digital world. Artificial intelligence is present almost in every digital space. Ever growing customers' demand for better and affordable products and services, quick delivery, best after-sales services, etc. are the need of the hour. To keep pace with this demand each business entity must adopt digital means to improve its overall system. Digitalization is nothing but converting the whole business into a digital world with innovation in productivity, packaging, after-sales services, etc. A better-trained workforce with the right choice in innovation will help businesses to be at par with this race. Consumers' self-gratifying requirements can be fulfilled through the opportunities provided by digitalization (Sashi, 2012). Consumers' experiences are enhanced with the help of it (Rigby, 2011; Weill & Woerner, 2015). It also amplifies consumers' worth (Rintamäki et al., 2007; Grewal et al., 2009) and is the main instigator for innovation (Lusch & Nambisan, 2015; Nylén & Holmström 2015). To survive in this demand- centric race, MSMEs will have to accept innovation (Eisdorfer & Hsu, 2011). Innovativeness in SMEs can be noticeably referred to as the process to promote skills up-gradation in every aspect of innovation (OCED, 2018).

The government of India took the bold step of demonetization with a formal announcement on 8th November 2016. A cashless economy through digitalization was one of the main aims of this move alongside curbing black money, eradicating corruption, eliminating fake currencies, and stopping terrorism funding. Through this announcement, notes of higher denominations i.e. Rs. 500 and Rs. 1000 were recalled back through bank deposits or bank exchanges. The government expected that this move will help in increasing the tax base as well as enhancing the adoption of better and faster technologies (Kohli & Kumar, 2016). The larger mass of the people of India depends mainly on cash-centric transactions where non-cash users are only 10-15 percent of the whole population. The ratio of currency in use outside the banks to the Gross Domestic Product is 11.1 percent, higher than many emerging countries (Ashwini, 2016). Even MasterCard in its report titled "Cost of Cash in India" has shown India using cash in about 80 percent of transactions (Ramakrishnan, 2016). Cash is also used immensely while purchasing online through the use of cash-on-delivery feature and it accounts for around 17 percent of the total sales (Morgan, 2019). We have experienced that the use of cards for payments by the consumers and the use of Point of Sale (PoS) machines by the merchants has increased after demonetization. According to a report published by the Reserve Bank of India, after both demonetization and GST implementation, the credit supply gap to MSME has widened to approximately $230 billion and it is same as 11 percent of our GDP (RBI, 2018).

After all the debates that spanned for over a decade, finally, GST was implemented from 1st July 2017. In simple words, it is a form of 'one nation, one tax', where almost all the state level and central level taxes merge to form a single tax system. This type

NMIMS
Management Review
ISSN: 0971-1023
Volume XXIX
Issue-3 | July 2021

of tax system is in force in almost all major economies. GST was helmed as one of the most important economic reforms post-independence. But, the implementation was not proper as was evident from the different problems faced by the businesses. As it was a completely unique and new concept for the industry, the complex documentation related to it and the initial high tax rates for many goods and services posed as a challenging aspect for every business. Credit claims and "complex or unclear treatment" of common transactions was not aptly defined or taken care of at the initial stage which added to all the woes that the industry faced (PwC India Report, 2018). Unavailability of raw materials was also a known issue in the initial days of GST implementation. It presented a unified India where almost all the barriers related to different state taxes were abolished and free movement of goods became easier across the different state borders. The movement of trucks became faster. It allowed easier and faster movements of goods across the state which in turn lowered the required number of warehouses in different states. The multiple tax rate slabs implemented by GST makes it more complicated (FE Knowledge Desk, 2018). According to a report published on the completion of one year of GST implementation, issues with compliances, burdensome registration system, formulation of new cess, and refund problems were shown as the major hurdles that the business faced (ET Bureau, 2018).

The third shock to cause a severe effect on the industry came in the form of Covid-19. The previous two were economic reforms but the third one is a pandemic that engulfed the entire world's economy. In 5 years, i.e., 2016, 2017, and 2020, these 3 major shocks took the role of a destructor or a constructor/opportunity giver for the MSMEs in India. In the case of demonetization and GST, business was slow but there was no complete business closure but it was completely different in this pandemic. Business closure became the need of the hour to contain the spread of the coronavirus. Businesses were closed to maintain the social distancing protocol being laid down by the government. To contain the spread of the virus, the Government of India initiated a series of lockdowns starting a 21-day complete lockdown from 25th March 2020. It was anticipated that the Indian economy lost approximately 32,000 crores per day during these lockdowns (The Hindu Business Line, 2020), the live industry's loss was around 3.000 crores (Goyal, 2020). Daily wage earners and the informal sector faced the hardest times during these lockdowns (Das, 2020). Revenue from Information Technology (IT) sector also felt a decline of 2%-7% in the initial days and this virus's impact on the Indian economy was anticipated to be about Rs. 8.8 trillion (Kumar, 2020). Tourism industries also took a major hit due to national and international travel restrictions (Muthukrishnan, 2020). We have yet to contain the spread of the virus till today. Airways and roadways are still not fully operational. Work from home or study from home is severely affecting our lives. Business is yet to be fully productive in terms of revenue generation. This pandemic has not only taken lives but also ruined families. Either the bread earner of the family died or

NMIMS
NMIMS
Management Review
ISSN: 0971-1023
Volume XXIX
Issue-3 | July 2021

the family had to incur huge medical expenses. Many businesses have closed down with unemployment touching record high. In these uncertain times, we are hoping for a normal life as early as possible. The usage of digital payments rose immensely for businesses selling groceries and pharmaceuticals products. Payments of utility bills online recharge and education through online platforms also witnessed a huge surge (Tafti *et al.*, 2020). Few positive effects of the pandemic- related restrictions included the increases of several activities on the online platform and the increase of e-commerce transactions (Dutt, 2020).

This paper tries to understand the impact of these 3 shocks from the root of the MSME sector i.e. the rural MSMEs. The role of innovation or the use of digitalization for the survival of MSMEs is being studied through this paper.

2. Literature Review

Our country is growing at a fast pace on every front. The current government is emphasising on 'Make in India' and 'Made in India' projects. This will not only increase the demand in the consumption perspective but also the employment perspective. With the growth in demand for better products at reasonable rates with the best value, innovation is becoming the only viable option through the better use of digitalization. MSMEs have the power to cater to both the above-mentioned demands. More the stronger the MSMEs will become the stronger we will see our economy and the financial status of the majority of the population. Reforms are very much necessary for a better working environment, but on the other hand, the support should also be there to cope with any changes. Maximum MSMEs are run by individual proprietors and they depend heavily on cash with limited cash reserves, small turnovers, and limited access to finances (Beyes and Bhattacharya, 2016). The impact of demonetization was therefore felt more by these small businesses that deal with more cash transactions. The Demonetization move was unexpected but this happened earlier in India in 1946 and 1978 (PWC, 2016). Four major reasons behind this bold move as given by our Prime Minister are: Firstly, the undeclared income would come under the radar of the income tax department. Secondly, the counterfeit currency would become useless. Thirdly, it will push the country to move from a cash economy to a cashless economy through the use of digital means of payment. Fourthly, it will help to generate more digital footprints to track the individuals in all the financial activities. This may also help the banking sector to strengthen its economic position. This has indeed increased the digital payments by individuals and is a positive step towards the digitization of our economy. But, this move has impacted almost every sector with auto sales going down by 4.7 percent, the decline in cement production, passenger vehicles also experienced a fall of nearly 2 percent, and the commercial vehicles sales also took the beating (Walkins, 2017). Among few studies conducted just after demonetization, there was a 46 percent decline in sales in

NMIMS
Management Review
ISSN: 0971-1023
Volume XXIX
Issue-3 | July 2021

Amritsar (Sibbal, 2017) and the decline of earnings by small businesses was nearly 45 percent in Ranchi (Lahiri, 2016). The other instance is of the small traders or business-related with retail sector being impacted in Ghaziabad (Vij, 2017). These bold policies of the government give a boost to several innovations including digital payments and people get a ping to use it to overcome a cash- related crisis (Bhuvana and Vasantha, 2017). This type of move can also help in lowering the interest rates of the banks and the influx of huge funds will help the development of the economic perspective of the country (Kohli and Kumar, 2016). In the initial days, many labours and workers working in MSMEs lost their jobs but were again reinstated after the initial jitters were over (Bhagat, 2017). The cash crunch being created by this step has largely affected those cash-dependent sectors including micro or small businesses as well as the cottage industry (Tiwari and Tiwari, 2017). This reform despite facing several problems still can be treated as a success (Midthanpally, 2017; Kulkarni and Tapas, 2017).The effect of demonetization was more on unregistered firms. Few firms used the mode of digital mode of payment but due to rare instances of the usage of it, they switched over to the normal mode after the turmoil was over (Kurosaki, 2016). Demonetisation caused acute disruption in the cash-dependent business sector and this lasted for almost 2 months. The result of this economic policy was the largest monetary shock that ever occurred in India (Lahiri, 2020).

Going by the recent turmoil, the coronavirus outbreak is the biggest challenge that the whole world is facing. We are yet to fight it out completely. Business, education, health, employment, the economy, and almost everything related to our life are being impacted by the pandemic. India's economy is projected to lose more than $348 million (Khosla, 2020). Manufacturing of electronics in China has dropped from 55 percent to 40 percent due to the quarantines and lockdowns related to this pandemic (Kumar, 2020). Even the education of almost 1.716 billion students is impacted and ' Online classes from home' has become a normal routine (UNESCO, 2020a). The number of confirmed cases of Covid-19 in the initial two months was more than the number of cases reached in eight months from SARS disease. It was declared a global pandemic in the 3rd month of the outbreak. Lockdowns were a normal phenomenon in almost every country with a complete shutdown of businesses in almost every sector. These lockdowns, on one hand, helped contain its spread but on the other hand a severe impact on individuals through job loss, loss of kith and kin, economic loss and loss in business which curtailed the production and revenues. As the manufacturing sector returned to partial operations sooner than the service sector and the loss is more in the service sector. The cash liquidity in 50 % of the smaller businesses is of less than 15 days whereas only 40 % have cash liquidity of approximately three weeks (Farrell et. al., 2020). A small business faces the problem more because of its poor level of preparedness, higher reliance on support from the government, and greater vulnerability from any financial or psychological impact (Runyan, 2020).

NMIMS

NMIMS
Management Review
ISSN: 0971-1023
Volume XXIX
Issue-3 | July 2021

Few of the past studies that highlighted the after-effects or preparedness or survival strategy of the businesses includes one of Phuket, Thailand. The study was conducted after the disaster in tourism industry and the author found that the savings of any business is one of the prime factors for their resilience (Biggs et al., 2012). Post-disaster recovery of businesses becomes one of the important aspects to fight with these uncertain times. Supply chain disruptions were found out as one of the factors after the Northridge Earthquake in 1994 (Dahlhamer and Tierney, 1998) and the East Japan Earthquake in 2011 (Tokui et al., 2017). The prolonged period of business disruption is the form of closure or interruptions in receiving or supplying raw materials or products that can also be a hindrance in the recovery process of SMEs (Tierney, 2007). After the recent SARS epidemic, it is found out that it mainly affected consumption and induced a demand shock. It led to an uncertain and volatile environment for those SMEs whose business got hampered with a change in the labour market or customer demand or supply chains (Lee and Warner, 2006). It was also found out that there was a change in purchasing pattern of the consumers with an increase in consumption of low-cost products (Liu and Black, 2011) and a decrease in consumption of luxury goods (Zhang et al., 2009; Forbes, 2017).

These economic reforms or the pandemic has sprung one important question for the industry, what does it need to survive in uncertain times? Nearly 53 percent of businesses in India were affected due to the lockdowns (The Indian Express, 2020) and these businesses are those having almost no savings or no cash flow for them so the support from the government becomes vital for their survival (Biggs et al., 2012). This type of crisis directly impacts the owners access to finance, their business strategies (Sonfield and Lussier, 2000), their approach to prospect identification (Pattinson, 2016), or their decision-making abilities (Laskovaia et al., 2019). They should always be ready to cope up with these uncertain markets and challenging operating conditions (Morris et al., 2008). With time, the burden seems to be getting heavier on the worldwide ecological system and even governmental financial reforms or advancement in innovations targeted towards sustainability cannot lower down these burdens (Cohen, 2020). Yet, support from the government is considered to be an important factor towards adopting technological business changes (Lin and Ho, 2009). After the devastation of the Rita and Katrina hurricanes, it was concluded that to rejuvenate businesses after any disaster, the government can devise tax-related incentives and help them through their reinvestments (Gotham, 2013). The financial bailout package that the government of India proposed during the pandemic was just 0.85 percent of its Gross Domestic Product (GDP) i.e. $22 billion. As compared with the United States or the European countries or other developed or developing Asian countries, this scheme was much lower. It should have been 4-5 percent or higher looking into the effect of the pandemic in the country (Mahendra Dev, 2020). The

NMIMS
Management Review
ISSN: 0971-1023
Volume XXIX
Issue-3 | July 2021

impacts of these discontinuous events are severe as it is difficult to predict the devastation it can create (Taleb, 2007; Turchin, 2008; Turchin 2016). These life-changing and stressful events create friction or alter consumption habits and this change helps them in managing the stress created by these events (Mathur et al., 2003). The ability to absorb supply chain disruptions by the micro-enterprises is less and they always miss out on getting any form of disaster-related aid (Prasad et al., 2014). The deficit in working capital is common with many SMEs (Psillaki and Eleftheriou, 2015; Lee et al., 2015). Businesses find it difficult to recover just after the pandemic with the continuance of their investments or with an increase in it as the consumption pattern just after any pandemic is uncertain (Joo et al., 2019). Small businesses in India faced the largest impact of the Covid-19 pandemic. Even the introduction of several policy measures could not boost their morale as they seemed helpless in the current situation. The government should focus on understanding the grass-root problems of the MSMEs and should try to implement the suggestions provided by them to revive this sector after the effects of the pandemic are over (Rathore and Khanna, 2021). The current situation can be tackled or handled with timely intervention from the government through their business-friendly policy measures (Tripathy and Bisoyi, 2021).

Though there can be uncertain events at an equally uncertain time MSMEs need to formulate an ecologically viable strategy for their business. Technology can help in this restructuring to deliver sustainability through enhanced production and consumption (Geels, 2014). In any kind of financial crisis, the innovativeness of SMEs is considered to be the key driver for their sustainability, growth, and competitiveness (Kakouris and Ketikidis, 2012; Kakouris et al., 2016). An entrepreneur, through the use of innovation in their business always plays an important role in helping and restructuring economy during or after the crisis (Devece et al., 2016). MSMEs adopt innovations mostly in their process because of the unavailability of a technically skilled workforce or the scarcity of required funds. But their adoption of innovation to face the challenges during difficult situations is quite evident (Sharma, 2017). Any uncertain event or economic reform can be interpreted as a hindrance or an opportunity for many MSMEs. The scarcity of funds or the high cost involved in current technologies sometimes inspires many entrepreneurs to take the business more competitively or sustainably by doing something different with their available resources (Sharma, 2014). Through the use of new techniques in producing new products to cater to the mounting demands of the consumers, technology innovation has become a necessity (Acs and Audretsch, 1990). Digitalization gives us virtual business opportunities in connection with the online business world having huge prospective customers (Worhach, 2000). The product-based business has been completely revamped to service-based business with the help of digitalization (Suarez et al, 2013).

NMIMS

NMIMS Management Review
ISSN: 0971-1023
Volume XXIX
Issue-3 | July 2021

3. Research Gap

Several studies focus on the post-disaster needs of the SMEs after the impact of any disasters (Tierney, 1997; Chang and Falit-Baiamonte, 2002; Wedawatta and Ingirige, 2012; Dahles and Susilowati, 2015). These studies have focussed mainly on the impact of environmental or natural disasters and recovery from them, studies on the impact of the pandemic are rare. The study on the impact of demonetization, GST, and Covid-19 related pandemic taken together are hard to find. The adoptions of digitalization for the business are different in the entire three scenarios, but it is difficult to find any study focussing on these aspects.

4. Objective of the Study

The basic objective of this study is to find out and understand the most important event that directly or indirectly forced MSMEs to adopt digitalization for their business to survive. The study will try to find out whether any of the three major events made the MSMEs think of adopting digitalization for their business.

5. Conceptual Model and Hypotheses

5.1 Demonetization Effect

The scarcity of cash during demonetization has boosted digital payment and has also increased the usage of online platforms for selling and purchasing goods and services in India. In long term, demonetization will show its effect on the adoption of digitalization in India (Lodha et al., 2018). Demonetization will help the government realize its dream of 'digital India' through digitalization (Paulraj and Sudha, 2020).

H1: *Demonetization effect has a significant effect on the adoption of digitalization for business*

5.2 GST Effect

GST is completely related to tax reforms of business. It generally made the taxing system of firms more uniform and its implementation was for each business for purchasing and selling of goods or raw materials. Still, it paved the way for the firms to adopt digital means to carry out their financial transactions for better use of GST reforms. The implementation of GST will boost the proper usage of digitalization by businesses (Sahoo and Sahoo, 2020).

H2: *GST effect has a significant effect on the adoption of digitalization for business*

5.3 Pandemic Effect (Covid-19 Effect)

Partial or complete closure of business activities during the Covid-19 related

NMIMS

Management Review
ISSN: 0971-1023
Volume XXIX
Issue-3 | July 2021

restrictions have crippled many firms. Loss in revenues has hurt businesses the most. They were back in business after the ease in restrictions. The restrictions and the fear of the spread of the disease have to lead many businesses to use or adapt digital means in conducting the business. Changes in the business scenario in terms of digital transformation will help the firms to battle it out with the effects of Covid-19 (Pedro Soto-Acosta, 2020). There is a surge in the digital transformation of business since the outbreak of Covid-19 (Almedia et al, 2020).

H3: *Pandemic effect has a significant effect on the adoption of digitalization for business*

Figure I: Proposed Conceptual Model

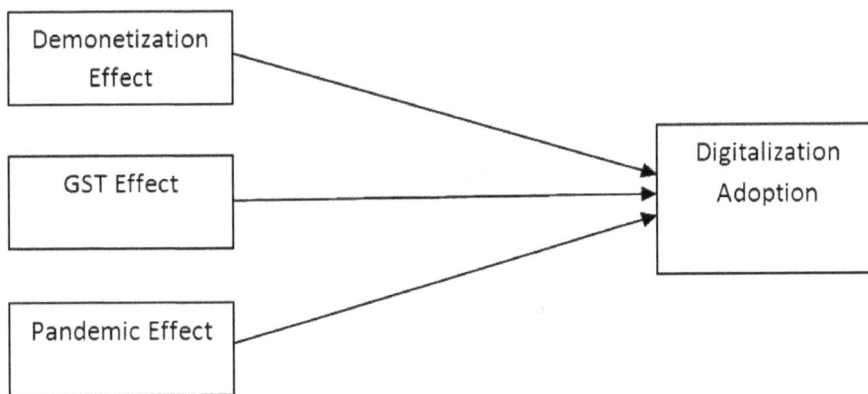

6. Research Methodology

In this exploratory study, both the qualitative and quantitative characterization of the research has been considered. Through a set of structured questionnaires covering all three events, the study tries to find out the main event which pushed the MSMEs to adopt or think of implementing digitalization for their business. Many multiple-choice questions under the four main constraints were provided for the response of MSME owners. All the responses were formulated on a 5-point Likert scale. The primary data were gathered through the use of an interview schedule (physically through field survey) and also with the help of Google forms in the online platform. The data were collected from 15th March 2020 to 15th September 2020. Among the collected data of 353 respondents, the data responses from 274 respondents were considered for the analysis required for this study. The data from the rest 79 respondents were either incomplete or repetitive.

For factor analysis of the data, the process of Principal Component Analysis (PCA) was adopted with the help of IBM SPSS 25.0. Through the use of IBM

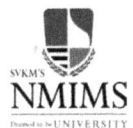

NMIMS
NMIMS
Management Review
ISSN: 0971-1023
Volume XXIX
Issue-3 | July 2021

AMOS 21.0, Structural Equation Modelling (SEM) was performed to find out the validity of the model.

7. Data Analysis

7.1 Demographic Profile

The total of 274 respondents included 94.2percent male MSME owners and 5.8 percent female MSME owners.

Table 1: Gender

Gender		
	Frequency	Percent
Male	258	94.2
Female	16	5.8
Total	274	100.0

The respondents were from different age groups with 33.9 percent of the total in the 41-50 years age group being the maximum.

Table 2: Age

Age		
	Frequency	Percent
Up to 30 Years	13	4.7
31-40 Years	77	28.1
41-50 Years	93	33.9
51-60 Years	83	30.3
Above 60 Years	8	2.9
Total	274	100.0

The following table shows the educational qualification of the MSME owners being surveyed.

Table 3: Education

Education		
	Frequency	Percent
Primary	65	23.7
Secondary	81	29.6
Higher Secondary	67	24.5
Graduate	42	15.3
Post Graduate	19	6.9
Total	274	100.0

The following table shows the MSME category, 39.8 percent in the services sector and 60.2 percent in the manufacturing sector.

Table 4: MSME Category

MSME Category		
	Frequency	Percent
Services-Micro	103	37.6
Services-Small	6	2.2
Manufacturing-Micro	145	52.9
Manufacturing-Small	20	7.3
Total	274	100.0

The yearly revenue as was revealed by the respondents (not verified through their Income Tax returns receipt) is shown in the following table.

Table 5: Yearly Revenue

Yearly Revenue		
	Frequency	Percent
Prefer not to say	118	43.1
Up to 15 Lakhs	123	44.9
16-30 Lakhs	30	10.9
31-45 Lakhs	3	1.1
Total	274	100.0

7.2 Data Interpretation

7.2.1 Sample Size

To have an ideal sample for the study of item-to-response ratio, the minimum and maximum ranges are considered to be in the range of 1:4 and 1:10 respectively (Hinkin, 1995). As per the standard, the responses of 76 to 190 respondents need to be considered for the study. After removing the incomplete responses, 274 respondents out of 353 were considered for the study. This lies within the range of above-mentioned ratio.

7.2.2 Data Analysis

To analyze the data, PCA was carried out using IBM SPSS 25.0. Before proceeding further for the analysis, Harman's single factor test was conducted to check Common Method Bias (CMB). CMB happens when "instruments are responsible for the variation in responses rather than the actual predispositions of the respondents that the instrument tries to uncover". A data is without CMB only when the total variance

NMIMS
Management Review
ISSN: 0971-1023
Volume XXIX
Issue-3 | July 2021

of a single factor is less than 50 percent" (Podsakoff *et al.*, 2012). The proposed study is not having much CMB as the total variance for a single factor of this study is 23.75 percent.

The calculated Kaiser-Meyer-Olkin (KMO) value and Bartlett's test of Sphericity values show the appropriateness of the data included in this study. The KMO value for an appropriate factor analysis should be in the range of 0.5 to 1.0 (Hair et al., 2006). The KMO shows the sampling adequacy and the suitability of the factor analysis.

Table 6: KMO and Bartlett's Test

KMO and Bartlett's Test		
Kaiser-Meyer-Olkin Measure of Sampling Adequacy.		0.779
Bartlett's Test of Sphericity	Approx. Chi-Square	3407.413
	Df	171
	Sig.	0.000

The proposed model elucidates 68.636 percent of the total sample variance which is more than the standard variance of 60 percent (Malhotra, 2011).

Table 7: Total Variance Explained

Total Variance Explained									
Compo-nent	Initial Eigenvalues			Extraction Sums of Squared Loadings			Rotation Sums of Squared Loadings		
	Total	% of Vari-ance	Cumula-tive %	Total	% of Vari-ance	Cumula-tive %	Total	% of Vari-ance	Cumula-tive %
1	5.175	27.237	27.237	5.175	27.237	27.237	3.592	18.907	18.907
2	3.724	19.602	46.839	3.724	19.602	46.839	3.451	18.164	37.071
3	2.348	12.360	59.199	2.348	12.360	59.199	3.103	16.332	53.403
4	1.793	9.437	68.636	1.793	9.437	68.636	2.894	15.233	68.636

All 19 items were distributed to form 4 components. These components were selected based on one or more eigen values. This can be confirmed through the scree plot which shows that the number of components for our analysis is 4.

Figure 2: Scree Plot

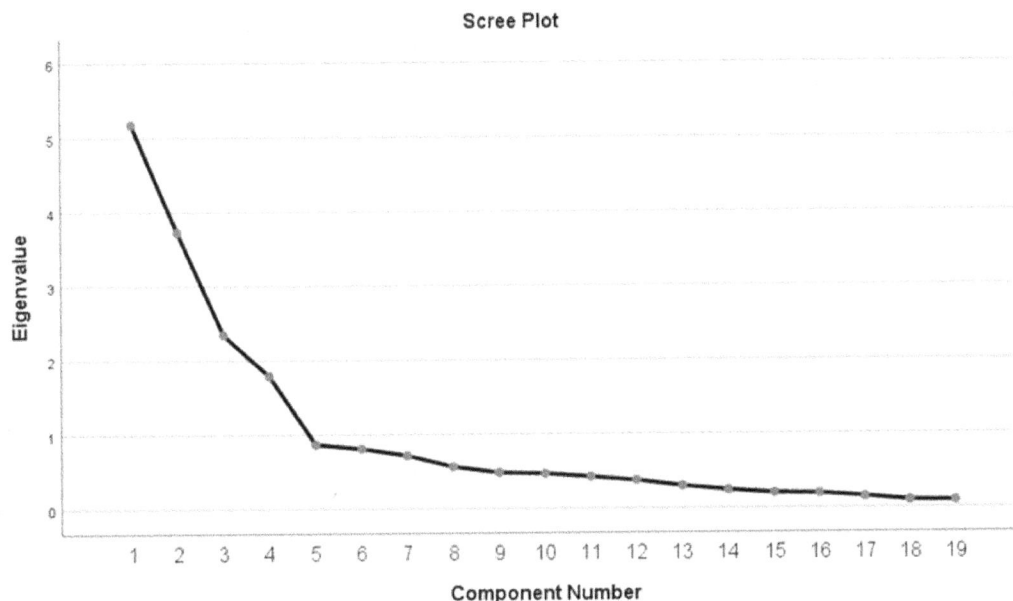

Cronbach's α value was checked to find out the reliability of the constructs. While considering the items for the analysis, a value of 0.7 or more is considered to be standard (Hair et al., 2006). The Cronbach's value of the total data is 0.838 which is above the standard value.

Table 8: Cronbach's α Values

Construct	Number of items	Cronbach's α
Demonetization Effect	5	0.885
GST Effect	5	0.901
Pandemic Effect	5	0.840
Digitalization Adoption	4	0.856

By using the varimax rotation method, a rotated component matrix is used to club all the 19 items into 4 components. All the items considered for the analysis had a factor score of more than 0.5 which is the accepted criterion for analysis (Hair et al., 2006).

NMIMS
NMIMS
Management Review
ISSN: 0971-1023
Volume XXIX
Issue-3 | July 2021

Table 9: Rotated Component Matrix

	Component			
	1	2	3	4
GST_Effec1	0.883			
GST_Effec5	0.873			
GST_Effec3	0.862			
GST_Effec2	0.852			
GST_Effec4	0.746			
DE3		0.825		
DE4		0.809		
DE1		0.808		
DE5		0.799		
DE2		0.781		
Pan_Effec1			0.839	
Pan_Effec2			0.761	
Pan_Effec5			0.739	
Pan_Effec3			0.715	
Pan_Effec4			0.710	
DigiAdop5				0.900
DigiAdop2				0.888
DigiAdop1				0.845
DigiAdop3				0.612

Extraction Method: Principal Component Analysis.

Rotation Method: Varimax with Kaiser Normalization.

a. Rotation converged in 5 iterations.

7.2.3 Data Normality

A normality check was conducted for all the items of the proposed study. It is one of the preconditions to conduct SEM (Byrne, 2016). The values of skewness and kurtosis for the items involved in the study must be below the threshold values which are three and eight respectively (Kline, 2011). It is found that the skewness and kurtosis values for all the items were less than the recommended values.

7.2.4 SEM Analysis

AMOS 21.0 was used to test the proposed model. In the SEM analysis, a two-step approach (Anderson and Gerbing, 1988) was applied. The first step involves the measurement of model and testing the reliability and validity of measuring scale using Confirmatory Factor Analysis (CFA). While the second step involves the testing of the structural model using SEM analysis. The result generated from CFA using maximum likelihood estimation is $\chi2$ ($\chi2 = 303.221$, df = 140, $\chi2/df = 2.166$), which is statistically significant. The fitness of the measurement model generated in our analysis is given below. The fit indices are at par with the accepted level needed for the fitness statistics.

Table 10: Model Fitness

Fit Index	Measurement Model	Standard Level
CMIN/DF	2.166	<5.0
Goodness-of-fit index (GFI)	0.897	>0.9
Tucker-Lewis coefficient (TLI)	0.940	>0.95
Comparative fit index (CFI)	0.951	>0.95
Root mean square error of approximation (RMSEA)	0.065	<0.08

To check the reliability of the data, the Composite Reliability values of the latent variables were generated. A value of 0.60 and above is considered to be good for a standard analysis (Hair et al., 2006).

Table 11: AVE and CR values

Latent Variables	AVE	The square root of AVE	CR
Demonetization Effect	0.55	0.74	0.85
GST Effect	0.61	0.78	0.88
Pandemic Effect	0.50	0.70	0.83
Digitalization Adoption	0.63	0.79	0.87

The average variance extracted (AVE) demonstrates the overall variance in the planned indicators. Its value is considered to be standard when it is more than 0.5 (Hair et al., 2006). As the AVE values are above the required standard, it indicates the convergent validity of the variables.

The discriminant validity (DV) among the latent variables is also found to be above the required standard. The latent variables are said to be having discriminant validity when the square root of AVE of each of the latent variable is found to be more than their correlation value.

NMIMS
Management Review
ISSN: 0971-1023
Volume XXIX
Issue-3 | July 2021

Table 12: Correlation Values

Latent Variables		Latent Variables	Estimate
Demonetization_Effect	<-->	GST_Effect	0.009
Demonetization_Effect	<-->	Pandemic_Effect	0.363
GST_Effect	<-->	Pandemic_Effect	0.09

7.3 Results and Discussions

The hypotheses of the proposed model are H1 (Demonetization Effect), H2 (GST Effect), and H3 (Pandemic Effect).

Table 13: Hypotheses Testing

Dependent Variable	Independent Variable	Regression Weights	S.E	t-value	p-value	Hypotheses Accepted/ Rejected
Digitalization Adoption	Demonetization Effect (H1)	0.151	0.066	2.296	0.022	Accepted
Digitalization Adoption	GST_Effect (H2)	0.06	0.057	1.053	0.292	Rejected
Digitalization Adoption	Pandemic_Effect (H3)	0.247	0.07	3.548	.0001	Accepted

The hypotheses of any given study are accepted depending upon both the t-value and p-value. For the acceptance of any hypothesis, the t-value is recommended to be within +/- 2 and the p-value should be below 0.05 (Byrne, 2013).

Demonetization Effect (H1) with a t-value of 2.296 and a p-value of 0.022 is accepted. Among the three economic reforms that have directly or indirectly affected the business, demonetization is considered to be the major one.

The scarcity of cash during demonetization gave a boost to the digital payment mode and also increased the usage of online platforms for the selling and purchasing of goods and services in India. Till the normalcy in cash circulation, the digital mode of payments was the only viable option. It was one of the major steps wherein the eagerness and benefits of using digital platforms along with the ease of using them, compelled both the consumers and businesses to adopt the digital means. Results indicate that demonetization has boosted up the adoption of digitalization and it has been justified by previous studies too (Lodha et al., 2018; Paulraj and Sudha, 2020).

GST Effect (H2) with a t-value of 1.053 and p-value of 0.292 is rejected. GST came into effect just after the demonetization. It is basically related to tax reforms in business. It

NMIMS
Management Review
ISSN: 0971-1023
Volume XXIX
Issue-3 | July 2021

made the taxing system related to firms, more uniform as its implementation took care of both selling and purchasing of goods and raw materials. Still, it paved the way for the firms to adopt digital means to carry out their financial transactions for better use of GST reforms. The results show that there was no significant effect of GST on the adoption of digitalization in business. It contradicts the previous study (Sahoo and Sahoo, 2020).

Pandemic Effect (H3) with a t-value of 3.548 and a p-value of 0.0001 is accepted. Partial or complete closure of business activities during the Covid-19 related restrictions have crippled many firms. Loss in revenues has hurt businesses the most. They were back in business after the ease in restrictions. The restrictions and the fear of the spread of disease lead to the use and adoption of digital means for conducting the business. Results indicate that the Covid-19 pandemic has forced consumers as well as businesses to adopt digital platforms to fulfil their needs. Digitalization was the only viable means to counter the restrictions as well as the fear of the spread of disease. The results indicate that the pandemic has a significant effect on the adoption of digitalization and it is evident in previous studies too (Pedro Soto-Acosta, 2020; Almedia et al, 2020).

The path analysis values of the data show that H3 (Pandemic Effect) has the maximum significance in the MSMEs owners' digitalization adoption process for their business to sustain the ever-changing market scenario with a value of 0.256 which is followed by H1 (Demonetization Effect) with a value of 0.157. The above two hypotheses proved that the owners were more reluctant to use digitalization in the current pandemic-related disruptions but demonetization gave them a push towards digitalization. As GST was implemented within a year of implementation of demonetization, so the hypothesis H2 (GST Effect) was less significant for the implementation of digital ways for the business. The results show that though demonetization was the initial major event that pushed the acceptance of digitalization for business, yet the pandemic effect gave a major push to it. Demonetization was a short-term effect where the cash circulation was back to normal after a few months of hiccups. But, the pandemic effect proved to be the worst nightmare for businesses as its effects were seen for a longer period with repeated lockdowns. We are yet to overcome the fear of this covid-19 pandemic.

Table 14: Path Scores

Standardized Regression Weights: (Group number 1 - Default model)			
			Estimate
Digitalization_Adoption	<---	Demonetization_Effect	0.157
Digitalization_Adoption	<---	GST_Effect	0.066
Digitalization_Adoption	<---	Pandemic_Effect	0.256

The path analysis of the proposed study is shown below.

NMIMS
Management Review
ISSN: 0971-1023
Volume XXIX
Issue-3 | July 2021

Figure 3: SEM Model

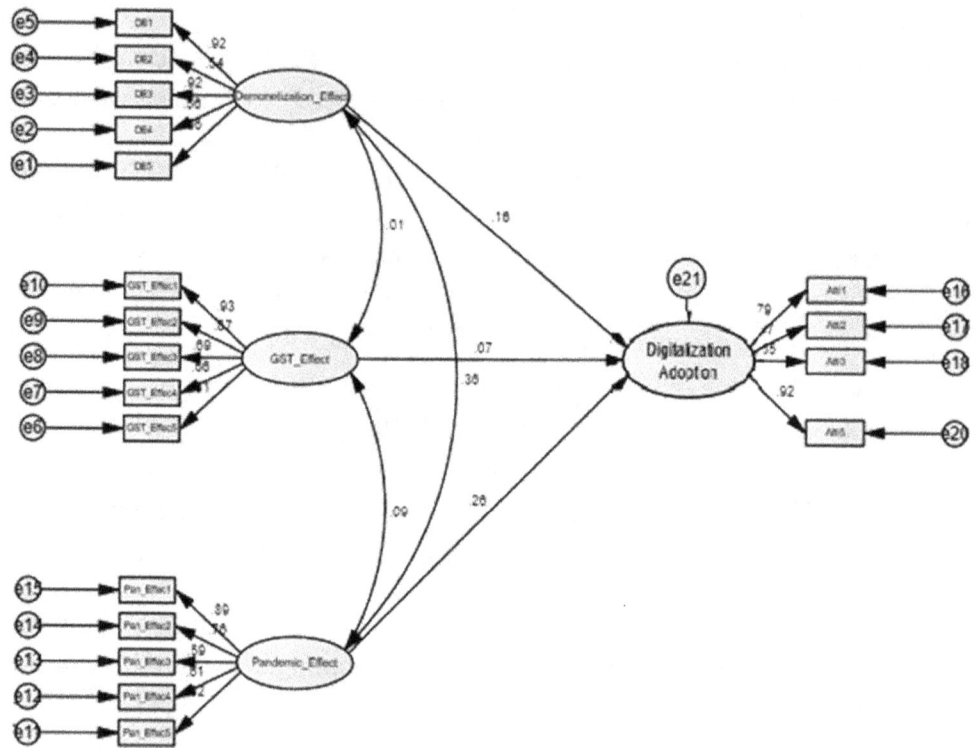

It shows the MSME owners have proper knowledge and understanding of the usefulness of digitalization for their business. It also shows that the recent advancement in innovations has made the use of technology in an easier way. The MSME owners perceive that digitalization is becoming user- friendly for them as well as for their business. The question that arises after the analysis of all the responses of the respondents is: If MSME owners understand the usefulness of digitalization and perceive it to be friendlier, then why the conversion from a non-digital platform to a digital platform is is taking a long time or why is the number of digitalized MSMEs are not increasing proportionately? The majority of the owners are dependent and looking forward to get the government support. They want real support and not reel support.

8. Implications

8.1 Theoretical Implications

The present market scenario demands MSMEs to be equipped with technology-driven products or services to cater to modern-day customers. With the increasing competition to survive, the need to adopt digitalization in business is increasing day by day. Digitalization gives us virtual business opportunities by connecting to the online business world with huge prospective customers (Worhach, 2000). With the

NMIMS
Management Review
ISSN: 0971-1023
Volume XXIX
Issue-3 | July 2021

help of digitalization, the product-based business has been completely revamped into service-based business (Suarez et al, 2013). The MSMEs have limited access to the latest technology (Ibrahim & Shariff, 2016). Also, they face another obstacle in the form of unskilful management (Arasti, 2011). The competitive advantage of MSMEs can be enhanced with the proper use of digital technology for business (Fauzi and Sheng, 2020). The optimization of "processes, managerial and strategic decisions, and customization" (Lumpkin & Dess, 2004; Watson et al., 2018; Kraus et al., 2019), creates various prospects with the use of digital technologies. In any kind of financial crisis, the innovativeness of MSMEs is considered to be the key driver for their sustainability, growth, and competitiveness (Kakouris and Ketikidis, 2012; Kakouris et al., 2016). To survive in this demand-centric race, MSMEs will have to accept innovation (Eisdorfer & Hsu, 2011). The results of the proposed study indicate that during all the three major events, the importance of digitalization has been witnessed by the MSMEs. These uncertain times have prioritized the use of digitalization not only for their survival but also to match the consumers' demands during those periods.

8.2 Managerial Implications

From the practical viewpoint, it is evident from the analysis of this study that MSMEs have understood the importance of adopting digitalization for their business. The government should utilize both these circumstances to push further their endeavour of 'digital India'. Both the events posed different challenges and hence proper schemes should be in place to counter the problems faced in both the situations. Digitalization will help India to fulfil its dream of becoming the 3rd largest country in terms of economy (Badam and Gochhait, 2020). The capabilities and performance of MSMEs can be easily and quickly enhanced through value creations with the use of digital technologies (Lumpkin & Dess, 2004; Nambisan, 2017). The success of 'Digital India' and the implementation of digitalization can be enhanced through better execution of different schemes and availability of resources in rural areas (Venkatesh and Lavanya, 2018).

9. Conclusions

In the last five years, MSMEs in India have faced three major disruptions in their business. In India, with the boom of e-commerce business and their services to almost every part of the country, many MSMEs are reaping the benefits while others are facing the heat from it. The local consumers are moving away from the local shops to virtual shops. The local shops cannot give too many alternatives for their products and also they cannot give large discounts that the consumers are getting through online shopping. Also, they are unable to provide multiple varieties of products, keeping the quality and the pricing intact as per the current demand. They do understand the need for them to shift their business from the old bring-and-mortar type to technology-savvy digitalized type. The three major disruptions have forced them to start from scratches.

NMIMS
Management Review
ISSN: 0971-1023
Volume XXIX
Issue-3 | July 2021

They are ready to change their way of running a business, subject to real support from the government. Relief from tax burden, intellectual and financial support, easy raw materials procurement support, more subsidies in electricity bills are a few of the important supports that they need from the government to fully concentrate on changing the way they run their businesses. They also want the government to prefer their products for use in local offices. It will not only increase their sales but also serve as a platform for advertisement.

10. Limitations

The pandemic-related travel restrictions have made data collection challenging and time-consuming. Also, many owners were reluctant to provide the data fearing that this may jeopardize their chances of getting financial support from the government. Given that a large number of MSMEs in India, the study could have been carried out covering more respondents but repeated lockdowns and lack of transportation means, have confined this study to a limited number of respondents.

11. Future Scope

Both the central and state governments are trying their level best to push the use of the digital mode of technology for business. But, there seems to be a gap between the cup and the lip. With the government's push for a "cashless economy", "Go Desi", "Make in India", or "Made in India" initiatives, this study and the further studies related to this can find out the reason for this gap. This will help the cup to reach the lip and both the economy and the MSME owners will be benefitted from it.

References

Acs, Z. J., & Audretsch, D. B. (1990). Innovation and small firms. Cambridge: MIT Press.

Almeida, F.,Duarte Santos, J., and Augusto Monteiro, J. (2020). The Challenges and Opportunities in the Digitalization of Companies in a Post-COVID-19 World, IEEE Engineering Management Review, vol. 48, no. 3, pp. 97-103.

Anderson, J.C. and Gerbing, D.W. (1988), "Structural equation modeling in practice: a review and recommended two-step approach", Psychological Bulletin, Vol. 103 No. 3, pp. 411-423.

Arasti, Z. (2011). An empirical study on the causes of business failure in Iranian context. African Journal of Business Management, 5(17), 7488–7498.

Ashwini, Sahoo P., "Here's what the impact will be of Rs 500, Rs 1,000 note ban: A massive change in informal cash-carry system to formal financing", Financial Express; 2016 Nov 10.

Badam, D., and Gochhait, S. (2020). Digitalization and its Impact on Indian Economy, European Journal of Molecular & Clinical Medicine, Volume 7, Issue 06, 2020.

SVKM's
NMIMS
Deemed to be UNIVERSITY

NMIMS
Management Review
ISSN: 0971-1023
Volume XXIX
Issue-3 | July 2021

52

Beyes, P. & Bhattacharya, R. (2016). India's 2016 demonetisation drive: A case study on innovation in anti-corruption policies, government communications and political integrity, Control Risks, New Delhi, India.

Bhagat J. New plans to boost self-employment: Shri Kalraj Mishra, PCQUEST; 2017 Jul 06.

Bhuvana, M. and Vasantha, S. (2017), "Mediating effect of demonetization of currency notes towards adopting cashless payment system", International Journal of Civil Engineering and Technology, Vol. 8 No. 6, pp. 699-707.

Biggs, D., Hall, C. M., & Stoeckl, N. (2012). The resilience of formal and informal tourism enterprises to disasters: Reef tourism in Phuket, Thailand. Journal of Sustainable Tourism, 20(5), 645–665.

Byrne, B. M. (2013). Structural equation modeling with AMOS: Basic concepts, applications, and programming. Routledge.

Chang, S. E., & Falit-Baiamonte, A. (2002). Disaster vulnerability of businesses in the 2001 Nisqually earthquake. Global Environmental Change Part B: Environmental Hazards, 4(2), 59–71.

CII, Micro, Medium & Small Scale Industry, Available at: https://www.cii.in/Sectors. aspx? enc=prvePUj2bdMtgTmvPwvisYH+5EnGjyGXO9hLECvTuNuXK6QP3tp4gPGuPr/xpT2f (accessed 31 May 2020)

Cohen, M. 2020. "Does the COVID-19 Outbreak Mark the Onset of a Sustainable Consumption Transition?" Sustainability: Science, Practice and Policy 16 (1): 1–3.

Dahles, H., & Susilowati, T. P. (2015). Business resilience in times of growth and crisis. Annals of Tourism Research, 51, 34–50.

Dahlhamer, J. M., & Tierney, K. J. (1998). Rebounding from disruptive events: Business recovery following the Northridge earthquake. Sociological Spectrum, 18(2), 121–141.

Das, G. (2020), "136 million jobs at risk in post-corona India", Livemint, Available at: www. livemint.com/news/india/136-million-jobs-at-risk-in-post-corona-india-11585584169192. html (accessed 31 May 2020).

Davis, Fred D., (1989). Perceived Usefulness, Perceived Ease of Use, and User Acceptance of Information Technology. MIS Quarterly, Vol. 13, No. 3 (Sep., 1989), pp. 319-340.

Devece C, Peris-Ortiz M and Rueda-Armengot C (2016). Entrepreneurship during economic crisis: Success factors and paths to failure. Journal of Business Research, 69(11), 5366–5370.

Eisdorfer and Hsu (2011) Innovate to Survive: The Effect of Technology Competition on Corporate Bankruptcy. 40(4):1087–1117.

ET Bureau, June 29, 2018, "One year of GST: The successes, failures and what's next on the agenda", Available at: https://economictimes.indiatimes.com/news/economy/policy/one-year-of-gst-the-successes-failures-and-whats-next-on-the-agenda/articleshow/64787124. cms?from=mdr (accessed 31 May 2020)

Farrell, Diana., Wheat, Chris., and Mac, Chi., (2020). "A Cash Flow Perspective on the Small Business Sector," J.P. Morgan Chase Institute.

NMIMS
Management Review
ISSN: 0971-1023
Volume XXIX
Issue-3 | July 2021

Fauzi, A. A., & Sheng, M. L. (2020). The digitalization of micro, small, and medium-sized enterprises (MSMEs): An institutional theory perspective. Journal of Small Business Management, 1–26.

FE Knowledge Desk, (2017)"What is Goods and Services Tax (GST)?", Available at: https://www.financialexpress.com/what-is/goods-and-services-tax-gst-meaning/1620322/ (accessed 31 May 2020).

Forbes, S. L. (2017). Post-disaster consumption: Analysis from the 2011 Christchurch earthquake. The International Review of Retail, Distribution and Consumer Research, 27(1), 28–42.

Geels, F. 2014. "Regime Resistance against Low-Carbon Transitions: Introducing Politics and Power into the Multi-Level Perspective." Theory, Culture and Society, 31 (5): 21–40.

GOI, (2020), Available at: https://champions.gov.in/Government-India/Ministry-MSME-Portal-handholding/msme-problem-complaint-welcome.htm (accessed 31 May 2020).

Gotham, K. F. (2013). Dilemmas of disaster zones: Tax incentives and business reinvestment in the Gulf Coast after Hurricanes Katrina and Rita. City & Community, 12(4), 291–308.

Goyal, S. (2020), "What is the impact of coronavirus on Indian economy?", Available at: www.jagranjosh.com/general-knowledge/what-is-the-impact-of-coronavirus-on-indian-economy-1582870052-1 (accessed 31 May 2020).

Grewal, S. (2012), "M-commerce and its growth: an analysis", International Journal of Technical Research (IJTR), Vol. 1 No. 2, pp. 32-35.

Hair, J.F., Tatham, R.L., Anderson, R.E. and Black, W. (2006), Multivariate Data Analysis, 6th ed., Pearson Education, London.

Hinkin, J.T, (1995), "A review of scale development in the study behaviour in organizations", Journal of Management, Vol. 21 No.5, pp. 967-988.

Ibrahim, M. A., & Shariff, M. N. M. (2016). Mediating role of access to finance on therelationship between strategic orientation attributes and SMEs performance in Nigeria. International Journal of Business and Society, 17(3), 473–496.

J.P. Morgan, (2019), E-commerce Payment Trends: India, Available at: https://www.jpmorgan.com/merchant-services/insights/reports/india#:~:text=Cash%20still%20takes%20a%20significant,17%20percent%20of%20all%20sales (accessed 31 May 2020).

Joo, H., Maskery, B. A., Berro, A. D., Rotz, L. D., Lee, Y. K., & Brown, C. M. (2019). Economic impact of the 2015 MERS outbreak on the Republic of Korea's tourism-related industries. Health Security, 17(2), 100–108.

Kakouris, A., and P. Ketikidis. 2012. "Editorial: poles of Innovative Entrepreneurship: A Triple Nexus." International Journal of Innovation and Regional Development 4 (3/4): 197–203.

Kakouris, A., Z. Dermatis, and P. Liargovas. 2016. "Educating Potential Entrepreneurs under the Perspective of Europe 2020 Plan." Business & Entrepreneurship Journal, 5 (1): 7–24.

Khosla, S. (2020), "Impact of coronavirus on the digital payments segment in India", available at: www.dqindia.com/impact-coronavirus-digital-payments-segment-India/ (accessed 31 May 2020).

NMIMS
NMIMS
Management Review
ISSN: 0971-1023
Volume XXIX
Issue-3 | July 2021

Kline, R.B. (2011), Principles and Practice of Structural Equation Modeling, 3rd ed., Guilford Press.

Kohli and Kumar. Economic rationale of 'Demonetisation'. Economic and Political Weekly. 2016 Dec; 51(53):31.

Kraus, S., Palmer, C., Kailer, N., Kallinger, F.L., & Spitzer, J. 2019. Digital entrepreneurship: a research agenda on new business models for the twenty-first century.International Journal of Entrepreneurial Behavior &Research, 25(2) 353-375.

Kulkarni, K.G. and Tapas, P. (2017), "Demonetization comparatistics: India and others", SCMS Journal of Indian Management, Vol. 14 No. 1, pp. 05-13.

Kumar, V. (2020), "Covid-19 and its impact on the Indian IT industry", available at: https://industrywired.com/covid-19-and-its-impact-on-the-indian-it-industry/ (accessed 31 May 2020).

Kurosaki, T., (2016). Informality, Micro and Small Enterprises, and the 2016 Demonetisation Policy in India, Asian Economic Policy Review, 14, 1-22.

Lahiri A.K. Demonetisation and the Cash Shortage, NIPFP, WP No. 184; 2016 Dec.

Lahiri, A., (2020). The Great Indian Demonetization, Journal of Economic Perspectives, Volume 34, Number 1, 55-74.

Laskovaia A, Marino L, Shirokova G and Wales W (2019). Expect the unexpected: examining the shaping role of entrepreneurial orientation on causal and effectual decision-making logic during economic crisis. Entrepreneurship & Regional Development, 31(5-6), 456–475.

Lee, G. O. M., & Warner, M. (2006). The impact of SARS on China's human resources: Implications for the labour market and level of unemployment in the service sector in Beijing, Guangzhou and Shanghai. The International Journal of Human Resource Management, 17(5), 860–880.

Lee, N., Sameen, H., & Cowling, M. (2015). Access to finance for innovative SMEs since the financial crisis. Research Policy, 44(2), 370–380.

Lin, C.Y. and Ho, Y.H. (2009), "An empirical study on the adoption of RFID technology for logistics service providers in China", International Business Research, Vol. 2 No. 1, pp. 23-36.

Liu, C., & Black, W. (2011). Post-disaster consumer coping: Consumption adjustment. In Yi Z.H., Xiao J.J., Cotte J., & Price L. (Eds.), Asia-Pacific Advances in Consumer Research (Vol. 9, pp. 214–221). Duluth, MN: Association for Consumer Research.

Lodha, M., Soni, R., & Vardia, S. (2018). Demonetization: A Push towards Digitalization- A Study of Udaipur City, Pacific Business Review International, Volume 11 Issue 1.

Lumpkin, G.T., & Dess, G.G. 2004. E-business strategies and internet business models: How the internet adds value. Organizational Dynamics, 33(2): 161-173.

Lusch, R.F. and Nambisan, S. (2015), "Service innovation: a service-dominant logic perspective", MIS Quarterly, Vol. 39 No. 1, pp. 155-175.

Mahendra Dev, S. (2020), "Addressing COVID-19 impacts on agriculture, food security,

NMIMS
NMIMS
Management Review
ISSN: 0971-1023
Volume XXIX
Issue-3 | July 2021

and livelihoods in India", Covid-19 and Global Food Security, International Food Policy Research Institute (IFPRI), available at: https://www.ifpri.org/publication/addressing-covid-19-impacts-agriculture-food-security-and-livelihoods-india (accessed on 31 May 2020).

Malhotra, N.K. and Dash, S. (2011), Marketing Research an Applied Orientation (6th Ed.), New Delhi, Pearson.

Mathur, A., G. P. Moschis, and E. Lee. 2003. Life events and brand preference changes. Journal of Consumer Behaviour, 3 (2):129–41.

Midthanpally, R.S. (2017), "Demonetisation and remonetisation in India: state-induced chaos or responsible governance?", South Asia Research, Vol. 37 No. 2, pp. 213-227.

Morris, M. H., Kuratko, D. F., & Covin, J. G. (2008). Corporate Entrepreneurship and Innovation. Cincinnati, OH: Thomson/South West Publishers.

MSME, GOI, Available at: https://msme.gov.in/know-about-msme (accessed 31 May 2020).

Muthukrishnan, M. (2020), "COVID-19 and its impact on Indian economy", available at: https://bfsi.eletsonline.com/covid-19-and-its-impact-on-indian-economy/ (accessed 31 May 2020).

Nambisan, S. 2017. Digital entrepreneurship: Toward adigital technology perspective of entrepreneurship.Entrepreneurship Theory and Practice, 41(6): 1029-1055.

Nylén, D. and Holmström, J. (2015), "Digital innovation strategy: a framework for diagnosing and improving digital product and service innovation", Business Horizons, Vol. 58 No. 1, pp. 57-67.

OECD. (2018). Promoting innovation in established SMEs. Available at: https://www.oecd.org/cfe/smes/ministerial/documents/2018-SME-Ministerial-Conference-Parallel-Session-4.pdf (Accessed 23 March 2020).

Pattinson S (2016). Strategic thinking: intelligent opportunism and emergent strategy - the case of Strategic Engineering Services, International Journal of Entrepreneurship and Innovation, 17(1), 65–70.

Paulraj. G., & Sudha, G. (2020). Impact of Demonetization and GST on Retailing Business, EPRA International Journal of Research and Development, Volume 5, Issue 9.

Pedro Soto-Acosta (2020): COVID-19 Pandemic: Shifting DigitalTransformation to a High-Speed Gear, Information Systems Management, DOI:10.1080/10580530.2020.1814461

Podsakoff, P. M., MacKenzie, S. B., & Podsakoff, N. P. (2012). Sources of method bias in social science research and recommendations on how to control it. Annual Review of Psychology, 63(1), 539-569.

Prasad, S., Su, H. C., Altay, N., & Tata, J. (2014). Building disaster-resilient micro enterprises in the developing world. Disasters, 39(3), 447–466.

Psillaki, M., & Eleftheriou, K. (2015). Trade credit, bank credit, and flight to quality: Evidence from French SMEs. Journal of Small Business Management, 53(4), 1219–1240.

PWC (2016), "Demonetisation – the long and short of it", available at: www.forbesindia.com/blog/economy-policy/demonetisation-the-long-and-short-of-it/ (accessed 28 December 2016).

NMIMS
NMIMS
Management Review
ISSN: 0971-1023
Volume XXIX
Issue-3 | July 2021

56

PWC (2018), Destination India 2018, available at https://www.pwc.in/assets/pdfs/publications/2018/destination-india-2018.pdf(accessed 31 May 2020).

Ramakrishnan, H. (2016), "Money with the bathwater", The Economic Times, available at: https://economictimes.indiatimes.com/news/politics-and-nation/demonetization-should-not-createinspector-raj/articleshow/55321528.cms (accessed 20 November 2018).

Rathore, U., and Khanna, S., (2021). Impact of Covid-19 on MSMEs. Evidence from a Primary Firm Survey in India, Economic & Political Weekly, Volume LVI, No. 24.

RBI, Demonetisation led to decline in MSME sector, GST dented exports: RBI study, Press Trust of India, Mumbai, Aug 17, 2018.

Rigby, D. (2011), "The future of shopping", Harvard Business Review, Vol. 89 No. 12, pp. 65-76.

Rintamäki, T., Kuusela, H. and Mitronen, L. (2007), "Identifying competitive customer value propositions in retailing", Managing Service Quality: An International Journal, Vol. 17 No. 6, pp. 621-634.

Runyan, R. C. (2006). Small business in the face of crisis: Identifying barriers to recovery from a natural disaster. Journal of Contingencies and Crisis Management, 14(1), 12–26.

Sahoo, J., &Sahoo, J. (2020). Challenges and prospects of GST in digitalised Indian economy, International Journal of Multidisciplinary Educational Research, Volume 9, Issue 2(3).

Sashi, C.M. (2012), "Customer engagement, buyer-seller relationships, and social media", Management Decision, Vol. 50 No. 2, pp. 253-272.

Sharma, N. (2014). Distinguishing Sectoral Innovation Behaviour: A Study of SMEs in India. YOJANA (Publication of Ministry of Information and Broadcasting), ISSN-0971-8400 , pp.56-60.

Sharma, N. (2017). Innovative Behaviour of Indian Micro, Small and Medium Enterprises: An Empirical Study, International Journal of Innovation Management, Vol. 21, No. 7 (2017).

Sonfield MC and Lussier RN (2000). Innovation, risk and entrepreneurial strategy. International Journal of Entrepreneurship and Innovation, 1(2), 91–97.

Suarez, F.F., Cusumano, M.A. and Kahl, S.J. (2013), "Services and the business models of product firms: an empirical analysis of the software industry", Management Science, Vol. 59 No. 2, pp. 420-435.

Taleb, N. 2007. The Black Swan: The Impact of the Highly Improbable, New York: Random House.

The Hindu Business Line (2020), "Covid-19 lockdown estimated to cost India $4.5 billion a day: Acuité ratings", available at: www.thehindubusinessline.com/economy/covid-19-lockdown-estimated-to-cost-india-45-billion-a-day-acuit-ratings/article31235264.ece (accessed 31 May 2020)

Tierney, K. J. (1997). Business impacts of the Northridge earthquake. Journal of Contingencies and Crisis Management, 5(2), 87–97.

Tierney, K. J. (2007). Businesses and disasters: Vulnerability, impacts, and recovery. Handbook of Disaster Research, Springer, 275–296.

NMIMS

NMIMS
Management Review
ISSN: 0971-1023
Volume XXIX
Issue-3 | July 2021

Tiwari, D.K. and Tiwari, D. (2017). Effect of Demonetization on Employment Generation in Micro, Small and Medium Enterprises. International Journal of Current Trends in Engineering & Technology, 03(05): 279-284.

Tokui, J., Kawasaki, K., & Miyagawa, T. (2017). The economic impact of supply chain disruptions from the Great East-Japan earthquake. Japan and the World Economy, 41, 59–70.

Tripathy, S. N., and Bisoyi, T. K., (2021). Detrimental Impact of Covid-19 Pandemic on Micro, Small and Medium Enterprises in India, Jharkhand Journal of Development and Management Studies, XISS, Volume 19, No. 1, pp. 8651-8660.

Turchin, P. 2008. "Arise "Cliodynamics." Nature, 454 (7200): 34–35.

Turchin, P. 2016. Ages of Discord, Storrs, CT: Beresta Books.

UNESCO (2020), "Education: From disruption to recovery", UNESCO, Available at: https://en.unesco.org/covid19/educationresponse (accessed 31 May 2020).

Venkatesh, J., and Lavanya, Kumari, R. (2018). India's Digital Transformation: Driving MSME Growth, IMPACT: International Journal of Research in Humanities, Arts and Literature, Volume 6, Issue 3.

Vij, D. 2017. Impact of Demonetization on Retail sector. International Proceedings on Paradigm Shift in World Economies: Opportunities and Challenges, Delhi, pp. 86-90.

Waknis P. (2017), "Demonetisation: Some Theoretical Perspectives", MPRA, Available at: https://mpra.ub.uni-muenchen.de/id/eprint/76391 (accessed 31 May 2020).

Watson, G., Weaven, S., Perkins, H., Sardana, D., & Palmatier, R. 2018. International Market Entry Strategies: Relational, Digital, and Hybrid Approaches. Journal of International Marketing, 26(1): 30-60.

Wedawatta, G., & Ingirige, B. (2012). Resilience and adaptation of small and medium-sized enterprises to flood risk. Disaster Prevention and Management, 21(4), 474–488.

Weill, P. and Woerner, S.L. (2015), "Thriving in an increasingly digital ecosystem", MIT Sloan Management Review, Vol. 56 No. 4, pp. 27-34.

Zhang, Y., Lindell, M. K., & Prater, C. S. (2009). Vulnerability of community businesses to environmental disasters. Disasters, 33(1), 38–57.

Shafique Ahmed is a full-time research scholar in the Department of Management and Business Administration, Aliah University, Kolkata, West Bengal. He can be reached at shafique1985@gmail.com.com, shafique.mba.rs@aliah.ac.in. His ORCID id is https://orcid.org/0000-0003-0983-8814

Samiran Sur is Assistant Professor in the Department of Management and Business Administration, Aliah University, Kolkata, West Bengal. He can be reached at samiran_sur@rediffmail.com, samiran.sur@aliah.ac.in. His ORCID id is https://orcid.org/0000-0002-8869-3547

The current issue and full text archive of this journal is available at https://management-review.nmims.edu/

Proposition and Validation of Retention Model for Managers in Select Indian Private Sector Banks

Niharika Singh ● L. Shashikumar Sharma ● Bendangienla Aier

Received: 16 April 2021
Revised: 14 June 2021
Accepted: 4 Sept 2021

https://doi.org/10.53908/NMMR.290303

Abstract

Purpose- Focusing on private banking industry in Delhi (India), the study intent to identify the direct and indirect influence of select individual, internal (organizational) and external (environment) variables on retention of bank managers. Three retention models for banking industry with the said variables had been hypothesized and tested to find that most appropriate model.

Design/Methodology/Approach - The required data of 301 lower and middle level managers was finalized using stratified random sampling. The managers examined for the study were with minimum two years of experience in the same bank. The study was conducted in two phases- (i) Significant determinants of retention were identified using multiple and hierarchical regression analysis, (ii) Involving only significant determinants three retention models were created and tested using Structural equation modelling (SEM).

Findings- SEM result of best fit model suggests that perceived alternative employment opportunities, perceived organizations prestige, perceived competitiveness of pay, pay and benefits satisfaction, career advancement opportunities, work-life balance, and job satisfaction have significant effect on retention of managers and the result is consistent with regression analysis of the work. Moreover, final model showed retention acting as mediator between other variables and retention, though the indirect effect was found to be very weak.

Practical Implications- The findings of the study will be serviceable for the banks want to keep those managers who had already spend a good amount of time in the bank.

Originality/Value- Rather than including two or three predictors, the current work has considered determinants of retention from various dimensions. The study extended its area by making an effort to involve only those who retained in the organization for two years and can actually have an opinion on the matter or factors affecting their stay.

Keywords: *Retention, Internal variables, External variables, Organizational variables, Bank, India, SEM.*

NMIMS
Management Review
ISSN: 0971-1023
Volume XXIX
Issue-3 | July 2021

Introduction

Retention of core competencies and talent is a challenge as it includes the mounting costs of retaining talent in the organization and the implications of failing to do so (Allen *et al.*, 2010; Mitchell *et al.*, 2001; Steel *et al.*, 2002).Dess and Shaw (2001) forwarded the view that turnover represent a significant cost to the organization, not only in terms of direct costs (such as, recruitment and selection, replacement, temporary staff, management) but also in terms of indirect costs (such as, pressure on remaining staff, morale, costs of learning,) and in the form of loss of social capital. Frequent shifting from one job to another is detrimental to employees' as well, as it requires transition in their self-concept (Ibarra & Barbulescu, 2010) and also has an affect on their families (Lyness & Judiesch, 2001).Thus, it is not surprising that employee retention and turnover has been widely researched for a century and continues to be of interest for academicians (e.g., Branham, 2006; Renstch and Steel, 1998; Vos & Meganck, 2007).Though research **on** employee turnover and retention has been prolific, there **is a lack** of shared understanding among researcher's conclusion on determinants of employee turnover and retention (Cotton & Tuttle, 1986).

With the beginning of 1990s liberalization, the Indian business environment has undergone remarkable changes (Sahu & Gupta 1999). And like any other sector, due to liberalization and constant growth of Indian economy, banking sector in India is facing new competitors from Indian and foreign based banks, which is tremendously enhancing employee's prospects for mobility from one organization to another. And as bank belongs to the service sector, the only asset for them is the manpower they possess because service providing organizations are not believed to have physical goods to offer(Ahmad et al., 2012). Where on one side, the banking sector is said to be the most employment generating industry and giving huge contribution towards the growth of the Indian economy (Setia & Singh, 2014), on the other, banks are facing a dismal situation of losing employees to new entrants. In recent years, a number of experts including HDFC bank's Managing Director and Chief Executive, Aditya Puri shared his anxiousness about the banks low retention rate mainly in private sector banks (I, II, III). The situation worsens with many new and payment banks exerting the market in recent years. Other than two universal banks, the Reserve Bank of India (RBI) had announced to grant payments bank licenses to 11 players in 2015 and has given in-principle approval to 10 applicants for small banks. Further, the competition is expected to get more intense after another in-principle approval of 10 applicants for small banks in 2020 (IV). To hire seasoned industry professionals for the growth of their operations, new entrants start to offer 100 percent salary hikes at the junior level and 30-60 percent at the middle and senior levels, strengthening poaching in the private banks (Parmar, 2015). However, in India, maximum efforts related to employee retention and turnover has been made

NMIMS

NMIMS
Management Review
ISSN: 0971-1023
Volume XXIX
Issue-3 | July 2021

for IT/ITES sector (e.g., Sengupta & Gupta, 2012; Tanwar & Prasad, 2016; Thite& Russell, 2010). Such ignorance of the banking industry in the past has motivated the present study.

The argument for the study begins with the words of Hom et al. (2012)' Everyone eventually leaves; no one stays with an organization forever'. This refers that the degree of insight gained from predicting whether a person leaves or stays is rather limited. Instead, the present study argues that predicting how late versus soon (i.e., when) an employee leaves and seeking for the reasons of stay occurring (i.e., why), can afford a more comprehensive investigation. As argued by Vandenberg and Nelson (1999), if one is aware of what is maintaining the stay of an employee, it can be predicted when leave intention might increase as a result of the organization overlooking a source that promotes retention behaviour for an employee. It is also said that one of the most vital steps HR practitioners should take when working on retention policy is to assess those retention factors which will affect their workforce (Steel et al. 2002).However, relatively very less research has given considerable attention to how an employee decides to stay in an organization and determinants responsible for the same (Cardy & Lengnick-Hall, 2011; Maertz & Campion, 1998).

The study is focused on determining pull-to-stay forces and create a retention model for experienced private bank managers with minimum of two years of experience in the same bank. After rigorous literature review, three groups of determinants were selected to verify their relationship with employee retention, where the first group includes seven individual variables, the second group includes four external variables and the third group includes nine internal variables.

As it is no longer valuable to simply link variable with turnover/retention, in fact, it is considered to be need of the hour to determine whether variables are causally linked to turnover/retention and how these links are moderated by other variables (Cotton & Tuttle, 1986). Thus, to analyse the relation between retention and aforementioned variables, in three groups of determinants, analysis was conducted in two stages. In the first stage, using multiple and hierarchical regression, significant variables were determined and in the second stage, hypothesized models were proposed with only those significant variables. The relationship established among variables to form the model was based on the previous research work and was tested using Structural Equation Modelling (SEM).

2. Research Framework

A number of prior researchers undertook similar efforts of including three or more groups as determinants of turnover and retention (e.g., Abelson & Baysinger, 1984; Huang et al., 2006; Min, 2007). However, the conceptual model identified by Min

NMIMS
Deemed to be UNIVERSITY

NMIMS Management Review
ISSN: 0971-1023
Volume XXIX
Issue-3 | July 2021

(2007) linking occupational, organizational, and individual variables with employee turnover, the effect of the aforesaid variables on job alternative and job satisfaction has been adopted in the study. The theoretical foundation is based on Zhou and Volkwein (2004) analysis of turnover determinants, where they included only significant variables from preliminary analysis for implementing SEM. If the history of employee retention is analysed, SEM had been often used by researchers (Riordan & Griffeth, 1995; Yang and Lee, 2009; Knight & Leimer, 2010). Individual variables have been introduced in the past as demographic (Thatcher et al., 2002-3) and personal variables (Cotton & Tuttle, 1986). In the literature, similar external variables as mentioned in the study were found under environmental factors (McBey & Karakowsky, 2001) or market factors (Huang et al., 2006). Internal variables were given under work-related factors (Cotton & Tuttle, 1986; McBey & Karakowsky, 2001) or further classified under job related/workplace factors and organization factors (Ariff, 1988; Pitts et al., 2011) in literature. The present study has combined job related and organization related variables and has named it as internal variables. Basically, the framework supporting the study has its foundation in four branches of literature: individual variables, internal variables, external variables and writings on retention/turnover.

Significance to individual characteristics of talented staff is fortified in the mainstream of management research by researchers such as Dries (2013) who underpinned in his work that 'attracting and retaining talented people is becoming increasingly difficult as a result of specific demographic and psychological trends' (p. 273). Moreover, in the past, individual differences have been identified as a potentially vital determinant for employee retention (Duncan & Loretto, 2004; Khatri, et al., 2001; Kumar & Arora, 2012) and turnover (Mitchell et al., 2000; Terborg & Lee, 1984). Therefore, in this study, seven individual variables viz., gender, age, marital status, number of dependents, qualification, level of management and salary were studied on their relationship with retention of employees.

Studies in the past included *gender* as a variable to examine the turnover or retention differences (e.g., Huang et al., 2006; Webb &Carpenter, 2012), giving inconsistent results (Huang et al., 2006; Stumpf & Dawley, 1981). *Age* is found to be significantly and positively related to intention to stay (e.g., Cohen & Golan,2007; Palomino et al., 2013) and actual retention of employees (Govaerts et al., 2011). Studies also show a significant effect of *marital status* on employee retention and turnover (Barkman et al. 1992; Huang et al., 2006). Only a handful of studies (e.g., Lee & Maurer, 1999; Sightler & Adams, 1999) examined the effect of a number of dependents on employee retention or turnover. Studies supported the argument that *education* is negatively (Kyndt et al., 2009) or not related (Govaerts et al., 2011) to employee retention. Seniority (*level of management*) of an employee is recognized to have a positive influence on retention (e.g., Govaerts et al., 2011; Van Hamme, 2009). Supporting

NMIMS
Management Review
ISSN: 0971-1023
Volume XXIX
Issue-3 | July 2021

human capital theory and efficiency wage theory, *pay* level has been verified as one of the most vital reasons for employee retention (Richardson 1994; Taylor *et al.,* 2010; Yamamoto, 2013)

In prior studies, a number of promising literatures have been studied and showed the impact of internal variables on employee retention (Hausknecht, 2008; Huang *et al.,* 2006) and employee turnover (Cotton & Tuttle, 1986; Mitchell *et al.,*2000). It concerns to the variables fully or partially under control of organization. The select internal variables for the study are monotonous job, employee training, work-life balance, workload, pay and benefits satisfaction, career development opportunities, job satisfaction, satisfaction with supervisor and organizational commitment.

Monotonous job has not been investigated much but kept because of repetitive nature of bank job. Price and Mueller (1981) stresses on the importance of routinization (or monotonous job) and Volkwein (1999) studied its relationship with employee turnover. Researchers advocated that *training* and employee retention have a significant and positive relation (Kyndt *et al.,* 2009; Bassi & Van Buren, 1999). Employees who have access to good *work–life balance* show positive employee retention (George, 2015; Gurunathan & Vijayalakshmi, 2012). Early studies focusing on *workload* appeared in the 70s (Guillevic, 1991). Literature on workload shows a significant and positive association between workload and turnover intention, partially mediated through job satisfaction (Guillevic, 1991).Studies proclaimed *pay and benefits satisfaction* to be only 'modest predictor' of retention or turnover (Ellenbecker, 2004). Literature proclaims that well-organized pay system has a direct and strong influence on the retention of human capital (Griffeth & Hom, 2001). *Career advancement opportunities* were cited as the most important characteristic for increasing the retention by Milman and Dickson (2014) and are considered to be more of concern to professional staff (such as managers) (Brereton, 2003). Studies highlighted the significance of *satisfaction with supervisor* on intention to remain employed (Dickinson & Perry, 2002; Gupta, 2011). The relationship between *job satisfaction* and employee turnover is one of the most significant topics in turnover literature (Khatri *et al.,*n.d) and is related to the expressed intention to leave as well as an intention to stay (Flowers & Hughes, 1973; Jayakumar *et al.,* 2009).Porter *et al.* (1974)claimed that *organizational commitment* (OC) was a better predictor of turnover than job satisfaction, which was supported by other researchers (Griffeth *et al.,* 2000; Kanwar *et al.,* 2012). Organizational commitment was also found to be related to intent to remain (Steers, 1977).

The extant literature supports the impact of external variables on employee's decision of staying or leaving (Birdseye & Hill, 1995; McBey & Karakowsky, 2000; Zhou & Volkwein, 2004). The variables falling under external variables are either under partial or no control of the organization. Further, it is stated by many researchers that no matter what a company does to keep the employees, they are affected by the external

NMIMS

NMIMS
Management Review
ISSN: 0971-1023
Volume XXIX
Issue-3 | July 2021

environment, especially when one considers retention (e.g., Hulin *et al.,* 1985; Idson & Valletta, 1996). This study considers four external variables related to employee retention, viz. perceived alternative employment opportunities, organization prestige, perceived competitiveness of pay and occupational prestige.

The significance of *Perceived alternative employment opportunities* (PAEO) is stated in the turnover model by Mobley *et al.* (1979), and the literature gives a contradictory result of being positively related(Thatcher *et al.,* 2002-3) and not related (Hulin *et al.,* 1985) to turnover. Also, PAEO is been mentioned as the most important factor affecting employee's decisions to stay (Hausknecht *et al.,* 2008). *Organization prestige* is one of the rare topics to be studied but a similar concept in relation with retention has been worked on, such as employer brand (Shrivastava & Bhatnagar, 2010), company image (Gupta,*n.d.*).

Perceived competitiveness of pay(PCP) is hypothesized to receive a fair salary which is equal to or more than the market rate and is a critical issue when planning to leave (Ghosh *et al.,* 2013) or to stay in an organization (MacManus & Strunz, 1993; Taylor III *et al.,* 2006).

Occupational prestige is not highly investigated in relation to turnover but as the population of the study is professional, the variable is selected to explore their effect, if any. And, some previous researches in the business literature has even identified strategies that link the image with an intention to stay (Latour and Peat, 1979; Oliver, 1980).

3. Research Question

To what extent the empirical data from private banks in India validate the theoretical model developed in the study?

4. Research Methods

4.1 Participants and Procedure

The data was taken from lower and middle level managers working for minimum two years in some selected branches of two Indian new private sector banks viz., HDFC and Axis Bank, located in the National Capital Region (NCR) of India- Delhi. The decision of including respondents only with a minimum of two years of organizational tenure was taken following similar kind of studies on employee retention, such as Rycraft (1994) and Vispute (2013) including employees only with two years and one year experience, respectively. As argued by Vispute (2013) it is necessary for an employee to spend some amount of time with the organization to provide relevant data on retention. The sampling frame had 204 branches for HDFC and Axis (122 for HDFC and 82 for Axis) located in Delhi, from which 60 select branches were sampled

SVKM'S
NMIMS
Deemed to be UNIVERSITY

NMIMS
Management Review
ISSN: 0971-1023
Volume XXIX
Issue-3 | July 2021

using stratified random sampling constituting 29.4 percent of the total number of branches in Delhi. Among these 60 branches, 36 were of HDFC and 24 of Axis. The uneven division of the number of branches for both the banks were sampled following the difference in the total number of branches for the banks in Delhi. To apply stratified random sampling, the Delhi region was first divided into four strata and branches were randomly selected (using random number table) from each strata; nine branches from each stratum (9 x 4= 36) for HDFC and six branches from each stratum (6 x 4= 24) for Axis were included. A total number of 333 lower and middle level managers from the select 60 branches were approached, whereas, a usable questionnaire was received from 301 respondents.

It is believed that the ratio of participants to items should be 5:1 ratio to be adequate for analysis (Gorsuch, 2003). The questionnaire in the current study had 37 items; so following the rule given above 37 x 5 = 185 respondents are expected to be a part of the study. Hence, a final sample size of 301 fulfils that criterion.

Self-administered questionnaires were used to approach the 333 lower and middle level managers, whereas 301 completed and useable questionnaires were returned, yielding a response rate of 90.39 percent, said to be an excellent response rate (Babbie, 2007). The questionnaire administered had three parts, Part I for background information of the respondent and Part II for eliciting the work-related/internal variables and Part III enquiring about external or environmental related variables responsible for retention of managers.

4.2 Measures

All measures except employee retention were measured on a five-point Likert bipolar scale with response categories ranging from strongly agree (5) to strongly disagree (1). For most of the constructs, reverse coded items are used which was recorded prior to analysis so that higher values indicate greater agreement like all other positive items. The measures have a minimum of three items, with Cronbach's alpha value of more than 0.70 (in pilot as well as main survey), which according to Cortina (1993) is the lower bounds for inclusion of a scale of measurement.

Dependent Variable: -

- *Employee Retention,*

  Employee Retention is defined as the employees' act of staying with the current organization for a recognizable period. Employee retention is operationalized as the time period for which current employees had stayed in the organization (or organizational tenure) and was measured using the statement 'Years of Experience with Current Bank'. Further, organizational tenure and similar concepts have already been used in previous studies (e.g., Joseph & Kalwani,

NMIMS
Management Review
ISSN: 0971-1023
Volume XXIX
Issue-3 | July 2021

1992). Thus, its validity has been substantiated.

Independent Variable: -

Internal Variables:

- *Monotonous Job (Cronbach's α = 0.74)*

Monotonous job is operationalized using three items, which consists of one reverse coded item. Here, an overall higher score on the scale refers to a low degree of repetitiveness in the job. An example of item, 'My job is quite repetitive(r).'

- *Employee Training (Cronbach's α = 0.71)*

The construct is operationalized using five items scale with one reverse-coded item. A higher score on the scale means training facilities are evaluated as satisfactory in the organization. An example of the item is, 'I get the necessary level of training from time to time.'

- *Work-Life Balance (WLB) (Cronbach's α = 0.75)*

To measure the construct four items scale was used using one reverse coded item. A higher score on the scale means the managers feel there is a good balance between work and personal life, working in the bank. A sample item is, 'Time-off policies are flexible enough to let me take care of my personal and family needs.'

- *Workload (Cronbach's α = 0.76)*

To measure the workload a three items scale with one-reverse coded item was constructed. A higher score on several items of this construct signifies that the work managers are expected to perform is reasonable. A sample item is, 'The amount of work I am expected to do is reasonable.'

- *Pay and Benefits Satisfaction (PBS) (Cronbach's α = 0.70)*

Those subjects obtaining higher scores on the scale indicated higher satisfaction with pay and benefits, within the organization. A sample item is, 'Bank is concerned to pay me what I deserve.'

- *Career Advancement Opportunities (CAO) (Cronbach's α = 0.72)*

Four items scale with two-reverse coded items was constructed, similar to Gaertner and Nollen (1992). A higher score on this scale refers to respondents have good career opportunities in the bank. An example of item is, 'On the whole, I feel I have good prospects of advancement in my job.'

NMIMS
Management Review
ISSN: 0971-1023
Volume XXIX
Issue-3 | July 2021

- *Job Satisfaction (Cronbach's α = 0 .82)*

To operationalize job satisfaction, four items scale was formed with the help of three items scale used by Lee and Bruvold (2003). The three items scale had Cronbach's alpha value of 0.88 for Singapore and 0.91 for US sample. All the items used in the current study are positive and strong agreement with the items means high satisfaction with the overall job profile. A sample item is, 'I like my job here.'

- *Satisfaction with Supervisor (Cronbach's α = 0.76)*

The five positive statements administered to respondents were inspired by a scale developed by Armstrong-Stassen and Cameron (2005). Higher scores on the scale identify higher satisfaction with the supervisor. An example of an item is, 'In general, I am satisfied with my supervisor.'

- *Organizational Commitment (Cronbach's α = 0.72)*

This measure consisted of five items similar to those used in other studies (e.g., Mowday *et al.*, 1979), with one reverse coded item. A high score on the scale refers to the fact that respondents feel attached to the organization. A sample item is, 'I really care about the fate of this bank.'

External Variables:

- *Perceived Alternative Employment Opportunities (PAEO) (Cronbach's α = 0.87)*

The construct was measured with four items where one of the items was reverse coded (negative item). Higher scores in the scale refer to the perception of respondents that a number of similar jobs are available and accessible for them. Sample item is, 'There are a number of jobs like mine available in the market'.

- *Organizational Prestige (Cronbach's α = 0.80)*

The measure consisted of three items and is a shorter version of the organizational prestige scale used by Hausknecht *et al.* (2008). Higher scores on this scale means the respondents believe their bank to have a respectable image in the banking industry. An example of item, 'Our bank is highly respectable'.

- *Perceived Competitiveness of Pay (PCP) (Cronbach's α = 0.78)*

The operationalization for this construct consisted of three items, where one item was reverse-coded. The respondents with higher scores tend to perceive that they are getting satisfactory pay possible in the industry for their job. A sample item is, 'Pay, I am getting here is fair enough in comparison to what other banks are offering.'

NMIMS
Management Review
ISSN: 0971-1023
Volume XXIX
Issue-3 | July 2021

- *Occupational Prestige (Cronbach's α =0 .74)*

Managers responded on three items related to the construct, where one is reverse – coded. Respondents those who strongly agree with the statements means to believe high prestige of the occupation outside the organization. A sample item, 'My job has a respectable social status.'

Individual Variables: -

Gender and level of managerial employees of the respondent was coded as a dichotomous variable. Age, salary per month and years of experience in the baking industry of the subject was operationalized as continuous variables; marital status, number of dependents and qualification of employees of the respondent was measured as categorical variables.

Control Variables: -

Due to possible empirical relationships (as established in past research) with the dependent variable, individual variables such as age (related to intent to remain, e.g., Finegold *et al.,* 2002); education or qualification (related to intent to stay, e.g., Dogan, 2008); marital status (related to likely to stay, e.g., Abelson, 1987); gender (related to retention, e.g., Huang *et al.,* 2006); number of dependents (related to staying, e.g., Sightler & Adams, 1999); level of management (related to retention, e.g., Govaerts *et al.,* 2011); salary (related to retention, e.g., Ewalt, 1991) were used as control variables in **the** latter part of the analysis (hierarchical multiple regression analysis).

4.3 Analytical Procedure

The study used the structural equation modelling approach used by Allen *et al.* (2003), Riordan and Griffeth (1995), Yang and Lee (2009), Zhou and Volkwein (2004) and suchfor validating the proposed model for retention. First and foremost, data were screened for missing data using the expected maximization algorithm of the missing value analysis. The technique was applied **to** age and salary with fewer than 2 percent of missing cases. Data was also checked for outliers, normality, linearity, homoscedasticity and multicollinearity to make sure that the data is appropriate for analysis. Scale scores for each participant were calculated by taking the mean of the associated items (Frenkel *et al.,* 2012).

The analysis started with descriptive statistical analysis, followed by Pearson correlation, multiple and hierarchical multiple regression analysis (Huang *et al.,* 2006; Vegt *et al.,* 2010). Prior to regression analysis, dummy variables were created for gender, number of dependents, marital status, qualification and level of management. To examine the relationship between the selected individual, internal, external variables and retention, five regression models were created (Huang *et al.,* 2006). Table

NMIMS
Management Review
ISSN: 0971-1023
Volume XXIX
Issue-3 | July 2021

1 lists the regression models used in the regression analysis. In the regression model 1, effects of only individual variables on retention were considered using multiple regression analysis. In Model 2 impact of external variables and in Model 3, the effect of only internal variables on employee retention was considered, using multiple regression analysis. In regression Model 4, hierarchical regression analysis was used and individual variables were entered in block 1 followed by external variables in block 2; to show the effect of external variables keeping individual variables in control. In regression Model 5, hierarchical multiple regression analysis was used and individual variables were entered in block 1 followed by internal variables in block 2; to show the effect of internal variables keeping individual variables in control. In Model 6, the overall effect of internal and external variables was tested, keeping individual variables in control. Thus, individual variables were entered in block 1, followed by internal and external variables in block 2.

Table 1: Regression models

Analysis models	Variables used		
	1	2	3
Model 1	Individual variables		
Model 2		External variables	
Model 3			Internal variables
Model 4	Individual variables	External variables	
Model 5	Individual variables		Internal variables
Model 6	Individual variables	External variables	Internal variables

Further, based on previous researches a conceptual model with hypothetical structural relationships was created, including only those variables identified significant in aforesaid regression analysis (Zhou & Volkwein, 2004). The proposed model was tested using structural equation modelling (SEM) with AMOS 18.0.First phase of SEM involves the measurement model. The measurement model is that part of the model which deals with the relationship between latent constructs and measured variables. Confirmatory factor analysis (CFA) was used to assess the measurement model, in which each questionnaire item was loaded only on its respective latent constructs, where all the latent constructs were correlated. The measurement model had seven latent constructs that correspond to four-item PAEO construct, three-item PCP construct, three-item organizational prestige construct, four-item work-life balance construct, four-item pay and benefits construct, four-item career and advancement opportunities construct and four item job satisfaction construct. As employee retention, salary and gender were single-item construct, they were not a part of the measurement model. Overall model fit was assessed using the maximum likelihood method. Several

NMIMS

NMIMS
Management Review
ISSN: 0971-1023
Volume XXIX
Issue-3 | July 2021

statistics were used to assess model fit, since sample size often affects the goodness-of-fit chi-square, several researchers have suggested multiple indices for judging the fit of a model to data (e.g., Marsh *et al.,* 1988). Therefore, the following indices were used in the present study to evaluate model fit: CMIN/DF, Goodness of Fit (GFI), Comparative Fit Index (CFI), Tucker-Lewis Index (TLI) and Root Mean Square Error of Approximation (RMSEA).

Once the measurement model created showed to have an acceptable fit, the structural equation model was examined to test the significance of the hypothesized paths between latent variables and assess the overall fit of the model to the data with several fit indices. In this stage, the hypothesized original model and other alternative models were tested and individual estimates for various paths were examined. Before testing the models, it was made sure that there are no outliers and no missing data. A combination of the goodness-of-fit indices was used to determine overall model fit. These indices signifies the extent to which a research model provides an improved model fit relative to a null model or independence model in which the correlations among observed variables are assumed to be nil(Bhatnagar, 2012).

5. Proposition of Retention Models

Regression analysis suggested nine determinants to produce significant variation in retention of Indian private bank manager's viz., salary, gender, PAEO, PCP, organizational prestige, work-life balance, pay satisfaction and career advancement opportunities.

5.1 Hypothetical Model of Retention

A hypothesized model was proposed including variables found significant and the hypothesized structural relationships between the significant variables which were specified based upon the cited literature.

This basic and initial model is composed of four components: exogenous (independent), intervening, endogenous (dependent) and control variables. The six (6) exogenous variables are indicated on the left-hand side in the model (Fig 1) with job satisfaction as an intervening variable (also act as endogenous variable). The model has retention as the endogenous variable, while salary and gender were control variables.(??) Based on previous research works, some exogenous variables have been hypothesized to have a direct relationship with retention, while others were assumed to have direct as well as indirect relations with retention through their influence on job satisfaction. The various exogenous variables in the given model are mainly perceptual constructs. These constructs help in the development of attitudes about the working situation. One collective measure about the attitude towards work is job satisfaction which makes it quite logical to use job satisfaction as an intervening variable. Further, previous causal studies in turnover (Bluedorn, 1982; Martin, 1979; Thompson & Terpening,

NMIMS
Management Review
ISSN: 0971-1023
Volume XXIX
Issue-3 | July 2021

1983) have hypothesized that all exogenous variables affect intention to leave only indirectly through the intervening variable.

PAEO was hypothesized to have a direct relation with retention based on Gerhart (1990). It means with opportunities in hand, employee starts comparing the current job with new opportunity and when he finds more cost than benefit for leaving the job, the employee stays. Based on Farrell and Rusbult (1981) PCP has hypothesized a direct effect on retention and the inclusion of job satisfaction as a mediator based on the link found between PCP and job satisfaction in literature (Thatcher *et al.*, 2002-3). Organizational prestige has a direct influence on retention based on Hausknecht *et al.* (2009) and March and Simon (1958). Work-life balance was reported to have an influence on job satisfaction (Vos & Meganck, 2009), which then influences retention (Friedlander, 1964; Porter & Steers, 1973). This gave sufficient evidence to create an indirect path for the effect of WLB on employee retention through job satisfaction. The placement of WLB in direct relation with retention was based on George (2015). Pay and benefits satisfaction was hypothesized to have an indirect influence on retention through job satisfaction and direct relation with retention based on Jayaratne and Chess (1984) and Shaw *et al.* (1998). Inclusion of career advancement opportunities with a direct path to retention and an indirect path to retention through job satisfaction was based on Pitts *et al.* (2011) and Zeitz (1990). Due to the establishment of a relation between salary and retention (Batt & Valcour, 2003), gender and retention (Mumford & Smith, 2004) gender and job satisfaction (Martin, 1979), salary and job satisfaction (Taylor III *et al.,* 2006), these two personal variables were controlled for their effect on job satisfaction and retention in the model.

Figure 1. Initial SEM model 1(Partial mediation)

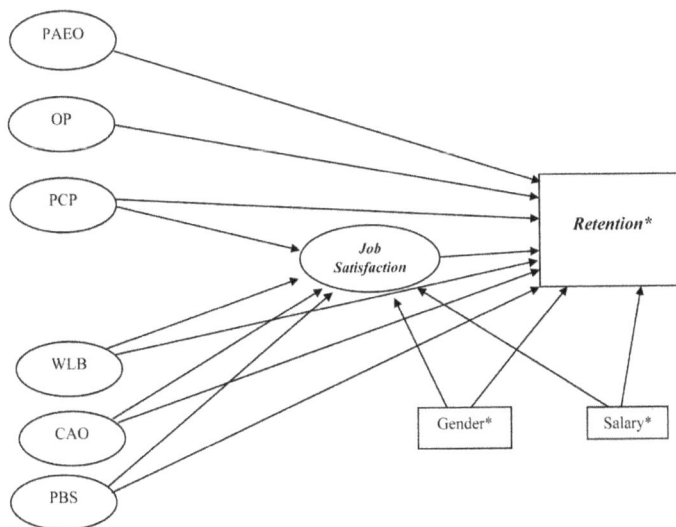

Source: Related literature

NMIMS
Management Review
ISSN: 0971-1023
Volume XXIX
Issue-3 | July 2021

Notes: PAEO= Perceived Alternative Employment Opportunities; PCP= Perceived Competitiveness of Pay; WLB= Work-life balance; PBS= Pay and Benefits Satisfaction; CAO= Career Advancement Opportunities; OP = Organization Prestige

*Constructs with one indicator or in numerical form are treated as measured variables, thus in box.

5.2 Alternative Models

There has been insufficient consistency between relations of variables/path in literature. It is not possible to predict clearly which variables would relate along a particular path. Thus, alternative models have been created and tested to include possible associations among variables. A fully mediated model and model with no mediator were also introduced and tested in the literature (Bambacas & Kulik, 2012;Liu *et al.,* 2013). In a fully mediated model, all the exogenous variables were hypothesized to have an indirect effect on endogenous variable through job satisfaction (Fig 2).

Figure 2: Alternative SEM model 2 (Full mediation)

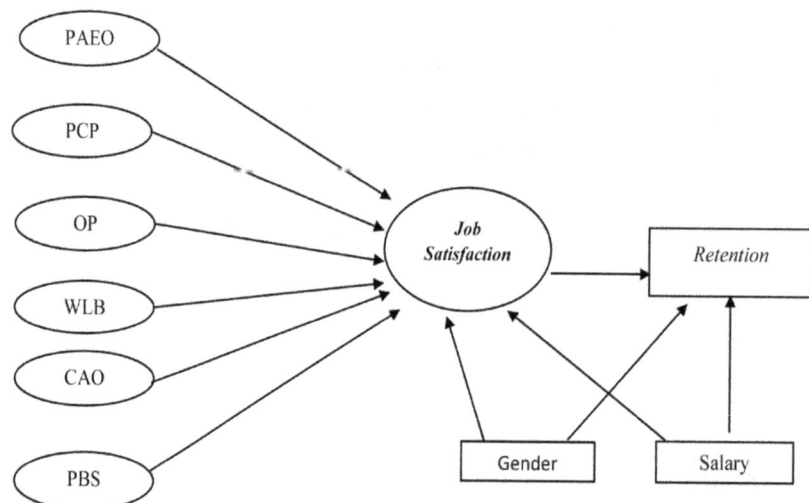

Source: Related literature

SVKM'S
NMIMS
Deemed to be UNIVERSITY

NMIMS
Management Review
ISSN: 0971-1023
Volume XXIX
Issue-3 | July 2021

Notes: PAEO= Perceived Alternative Employment Opportunities; PCP= Perceived Competitiveness of Pay; WLB= Work-life balance; PBS= Pay and Benefits Satisfaction; CAO= Career Advancement Opportunities; OP = Organization Prestige

Whereas, in model with no mediator considered job satisfaction as an exogenous variable and all the variables directly influencing endogenous variable (Fig 3).

Figure 3: Alternative SEM model 3 (no mediation)

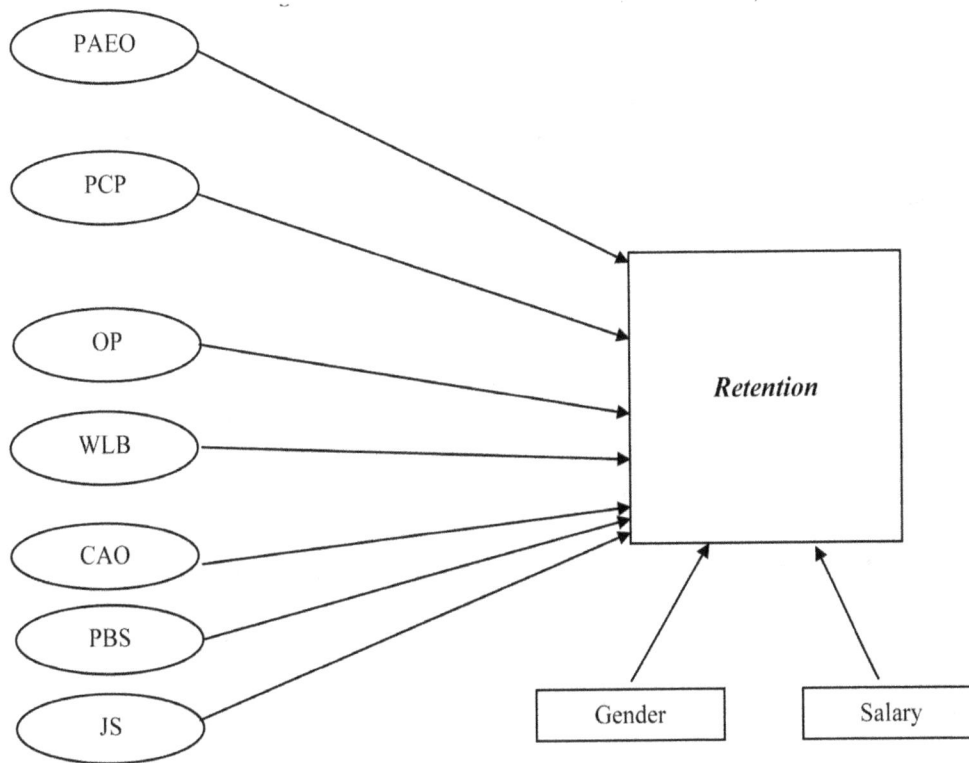

Source: Related literature

Notes: PAEO= Perceived Alternative Employment Opportunities; PCP= Perceived Competitiveness of Pay; WLB= Work-life balance; PBS= Pay and Benefits Satisfaction; CAO= Career Advancement Opportunities; OP = Organization Prestige; JS = Job Satisfaction

6. Results

6.1 Preliminary Analysis Result

Descriptive Statistics and Correlations:-

Means, standard deviations of independent variables and Pearson correlations between the independent and dependent variables are reported in Table 2. In mean value of the variables, organizational commitment is the highest (4.01) and PCP has the lowest mean value (3.47). Furthermore, significant correlation coefficients range from 0.12 to 0.80. Most of the correlations were, as expected, significant and positive which indicates that retention increases with increase in the level of those variables, except correlation between retention and PAEO ($r = -0.40, p < 0.001$). This refers that with increase in perceived job alternatives in the external environment

NMIMS

NMIMS
Management Review
ISSN: 0971-1023
Volume XXIX
Issue-3 | July 2021

length of retention goes down. The results, however, show no statistically significant relationship between employee training and retention.

Gender, marital status, number of dependents, qualification and level of management were treated as dummy variables. Thus, the correlations for those variables mean that females stay longer than males; married employees had been in the firm for a longer period than single; in case of number of the dependents, employees with no (nil) dependents stay for a shorter period and employees with 1-3 and 4-6 number of dependents stay in the organization for a long. Considering education, post graduates do not stay for long but those with a professional degree, such as MBA retains longer; employees from the middle level of management had been in bank longer than the lower level of management. But the correlations of age and salary with retention indicate that older employees stayed longer in the bank and an increase in salary enhances retention of employees.

Table 2: Means, Standard Deviations and Correlations for Individual, Internal and External Variables

Variables	Means	Standard Deviations	Correlations[#]
Gender			0.12*
Age		0.63***	
Marital Status(married)			0.48***
Number of Dependants (nil)			-0.24***
Number of Dependents 1-3			0.15**
Number of Dependents 4-6			0.18**
Graduation			-0.06NS
Post-Graduation			-0.24***
Professional/Technical			0.25***
Others			0.08NS
Level of Management (middle)			0.65***
Salary			0.74***
PAEO	3.82	0.35	0.51***
Organizational Prestige	3.75	0.50	0.79***
PCP	3.47	0.48	0.74***
Occupational Prestige	3.74	0.42	0.47***
Monotonous Job	3.55	0.39	0.68***
Employee Training	3.95	0.83	0.04NS
WLB	3.85	0.38	0.80***
Workload	3.58	0.47	0.66***
PBS3.48 CAO	3.81	0.38	0.80***
Supervisor satisfaction	3.49	0.38	0.79***
Job Satisfaction	3.82	0.40	0.20***
Organizational Commitment	4.01	0.47	0.74***
		0.36	0.73***

Source: Researcher's calculation

NMIMS
Management Review
ISSN: 0971-1023
Volume XXIX
Issue-3 | July 2021

Notes: PAEO= Perceived Alternative Employment Opportunities; PCP= Perceived Competitiveness of Pay; WLB= Work-life balance; PBS= Pay and Benefits Satisfaction; CAO= Career Advancement Opportunities.

*$p < 0.05$; **$p < 0.01$; ***$p < 0.00$*

#*Correlations are between the given variable and employee retention*

6.2 Regression Analysis

All six regression models met the assumptions of multi colinearity and outliers and there were no serious violations found in the plots of standardized residual against the standardized predicted value while checking for homoscedasticity, linearity and normality. To address the issue of multicollinearity, variance inflation factor (VIF) was examined for all the models reported in Table 3. Variance inflation factor (VIF) for the models ranged between 1.02 and 4.54, far below the allowable maximum of 10 (Neter *et al.,* 1989).

As evident from the result (Table 3), all six regression models examining overall effect of individual, internal and external variables on retention was found statistically significant($F= 4.91$, $p < 0.001$, Model 1; $F = 41.05$, $p < 0.001$, Model 2; $F= 30.12$, $p < 0.001$, Model 3; $F= 15.26$, $p < 0.001$, Model 4; $F= 16.61$, $p < 0.001$, Model 5; $F= 26.32$, $p < 0.001$, Model 6). This indicates that either all or at least one variable in each model has significant relationship with the employee's retention.

Next, to identify those significant variables responsible for the significance of the respective models, the individual effect of variables in each model was examined. While investigating effect of demographic variables on retention in Model 1, 4, 5 and 6, it was found that only gender and salary were significantly and positively related to employee's retention and the result was consistent in majority of the models. For internal variables examined in Model 3, 5 and 6, pay and benefits satisfaction, work-life balance, career and advancement opportunities and job satisfaction are associated significantly and positively with employee retention. The result is in agreement in all the three regression models. Whereas, from external variables, PAEO was significantly and negatively related to retention; organizational prestige and PCP were found significantly and positively related to retention in Model 2, 4 and 6. The result was consistent in the aforesaid regression models.

NMIMS
Management Review
ISSN: 0971-1023
Volume XXIX
Issue-3 | July 2021

Table 3. Multiple and Hierarchical Regression Results

Variables	Model 1 β	Model 2 β	Model 3 β	Model 4 β	Model 5 β	Model 6 β
Individual Variables (Control Variables)						
Gender (Female)	0.13***			0.01	0.03*	0.04*
Age	0.00			-0.10*	-0.07	0.01
Salary	0.59***			0.24***	0.12*	0.11**
Marital Status (Married)	0.08			-0.01	0.01	0.00
Number of Dependents1-3	0.03			-0.00	0.00	0.00
Number of Dependents4-6	-0.02			-0.01	0.01	-0.00
Post-Graduation	-0.01			0.00	0.03	0.03
Professional	0.08			-0.00	0.02	0.01
Others	0.05			-0.00	0.05*	0.02
Level of Management	0.08			-0.07*	0.02	0.02
External Variables						
PAEO		-0.08**		-0.09**		-0.09***
Organizational Prestige		0.60***		0.60***		0.35***
PCP		0.41***		0.37***		0.09**
Occupational Prestige		0.04*		0.04		0.00
Internal Variables						
Monotonous Job			0.00		-0.21	-0.28
Employee Training			-0.02		-0.00	-0.00
WLB			0.21***		0.21***	0.17**
Workload			0.03		-0.03	-0.02
PBS			0.41***		0.42***	0.27***
CAO			0.36***		0.40***	0.28***
Job Satisfaction			0.12**		0.12**	0.06*
Supervisor Satisfaction			0.03		0.03	0.01
Organizational Commitment			-0.05		-0.05	-0.06
Multiple R	0.51	0.76	0.80	0.79	0.83	0.87
R^2	0.34	0.62	0.71	0.63	0.74	0.80
Adjusted R^2	0.32	0.61	0.70	0.63	0.73	0.80
F	4.91***	41.05***	30.12***	15.26***	16.61***	26.32***

Source: Researcher's calculation

NMIMS
Management Review
ISSN: 0971-1023
Volume XXIX
Issue-3 | July 2021

Notes: WLB= Work-life balance; PBS= Pay and Benefits Satisfaction; CAO= Career Advancement Opportunities

*p < 0.05; **p < 0.01; ***p < 0.001*

Dummy variables coding- Gender: Male = 0, Female =1; Marital status: Single = 0, Married = 1; Number of dependents: nil=0, 1-3= 1, 4-6 =1; Qualification: Graduation = 0, Post-graduation = 1, Professional =1, Others =1, Level of Management: Lower = 0, Middle = 1.

6.4 Evaluation of Postulated Retention Models

For the main hypothesized proposed causal model of retention, degree of freedom was 1, this means model is 'over-identified' and 'one piece of information' was left for testing the model. In addition, all others alternative models were 'over-identified' as well, thus suitable **for further** analysis.

6.5 Measurement Model

Here, the estimation of overall measurement model fit is discovered, using various goodness of fit indices. Except for RMSEA, all other goodness-of-fit statistics showed a recommended level of fit, where χ^2/df (CMIN/DF) = 2.98; GFI = 0.93; CFI = 0.94; TLI = 0.95 and RMSEA = 0.08. RMSEA is a measure of the average standardized residual per degree of freedom; a value below 0.05 is considered good fit but values up to 0.08 is believed reasonable errors of approximation (Byrne, 2001). However, with four out of five indices indicating good fit in the model, the model reached the thresholds for indication of good model fit and is considered further.

To assess the model further, besides model fit, factor loadings of each item on their construct were measured. The CFA of the measurement model indicates that each factor loading of indicators was statistically significant ($p< 0.001$). Therefore, this is sufficient evidence of convergent validity for constructs in the confirmatory factor analysis (Rahman & Nas, 2013). Table 4 presents the factor loadings as well as squared multiple correlations for each indicator and standard error and t-value are given for statistically significant path. Squared multiple correlations (SMC) are interpreted as the percent of variation in any particular item, for which a construct is responsible.

NMIMS

**NMIMS
Management Review**
ISSN: 0971-1023
Volume XXIX
Issue-3 | July 2021

Table 4: Measurement Model Result

Latent variables	Items/ indicators	Standardized factor loadings(λ)	Standard Error	t-value	Squared multiple correlations
PAEO	Item 1	0.46***	0.12	6.37	0.21
	Item 2	0.42***	0.12	5.44	0.18
	Item 3	0.57***	-	-	0.33
	Item 4	0.44***	0.12	6.21	0.19
PCP	Item 5	0.56***	0.06	10.55	0.31
	Item 6	0.76***	0.06	15.19	0.58
	Item 7	0.78***	-	-	0.61
Organization Prestige	Item 8	0.53***	0.06	9.85	0.29
	Item 9	0.67***	0.07	12.39	0.45
	Item 10	0.72***	-	-	0.53
WLB	Item 11	0.39***	0.12	5.84	0.08
	Item 12	0.50***	-	-	0.25
	Item 13	0.54***	0.12	8.94	0.29
	Item 14	0.51***	0.13	8.11	0.26
PBS	Item 15	0.42***	0.06	7.98	0.17
	Item 16	0.62***	0.07	11.01	0.39
	Item 17	0.69***	0.06	14.39	0.48
	Item 18	0.70***	-	-	0.49
CAO	Item 19	0.58***	0.06	10.90	0.34
	Item 20	0.50***	0.05	9.51	0.25
	Item 21	0.69***	-	-	0.48
	Item 22	0.67***	0.07	12.36	0.45
Job Satisfaction	Item 23	0.38***	0.05	6.85	0.15
	Item 24	0.56***	0.08	9.92	0.31
	Item 25	0.71***	-	-	0.50
	Item 26	0.60***	0.06	10.68	0.36

Source: Researcher's calculation

Notes: PAEO= Perceived Alternative Employment Opportunities; PCP= Perceived Competitiveness of Pay; WLB= Work-life balance; PBS= Pay and Benefits Satisfaction; CAO= Career Advancement Opportunities.

***p < 0.001

6.6 Structural Model

From Table 5, it is evident that the hypothesized original model (partially mediated) had poor structural model fit (χ^2/df = 16.51, GFI = 0.86, CFI = 0.87, TLI = 0.63 and RMSEA = 0.29), whereas examination of modification indices indicated addition of an indirect path between organizational prestige and retention through job satisfaction could improve model fit. In addition, insignificant regression estimates between control variables and endogenous variables indicated that model fit could be improved by removing paths between control variables and retention or job satisfaction. Hence, following Zhou and Volkwein (2004), they were dropped out. The re-specified model had good overall model fit (χ^2/df = 2.10, GFI = 0.99, CFI = 1.00, TLI = 0.98 and RMSEA = 0.06). This indicates that organizational prestige affects retention directly as well as indirectly through job satisfaction.

In full mediation model, all exogenous variables are affecting on retention through their effect on job satisfaction. The model was a poor fit (χ^2/df = 47. 65, GFI = 0.78, CFI = 0.71, TLI = 0.33 and RMSEA = 0.39) and after the modification re-specified model was still a poor fit (χ^2/df = 59.25, GFI = 0.76, CFI = 0.71, TLI = 0.22 and RMSEA = 0.47) (Table 5).

An alternative model with no mediator, all exogenous variables are directly affecting retention with no mediator in between. The goodness-of-fit indices were poor (χ^2/df = 25.02, GFI = 0.87, CFI = 0.88, TLI = 0.65 and RMSEA = 0.18). After examination of modification indices, no much help was found but paths with insignificant regression estimates were removed and re-specified model was better fit than initial model but not the best of all. (χ^2/df = 16.02, GFI = 0.90, CFI = 0.91, TLI = 0.71 and RMSEA = 0.08).

These results suggest that the re-specified original hypothesized (partial mediated) model has the best model fit and can be accepted as the final model for retention of managers in selected Indian private sector banks (Table 5).

Table 5: Summary of fit index results (SEM)

Models	df	Model fit indices				
		χ^2/df	GFI	CFI	TLI	RMSEA
SEM model 1 (Partial mediation)						
(Initial model)	1	16.51	0.86	0.87	0.63	0.29
(Re-specified model)	1	2.10	0.99	1.00	0.98	0.06
SEM model 2 (Full mediation)						
(Initial model)	19	47.65	0.78	0.71	0.33	0.39
(Re-specified model)	13	59.25	0.76	0.71	0.22	0.47
SEM model 3 (No mediation)						
(Initial model)	15	25.02	0.87	0.88	0.65	0.18
(Re-specified model)	13	16.02	0.90	0.91	0.71	0.08

Source: Researcher's calculation

Figure 4. Final (re-specified) SEM model 1

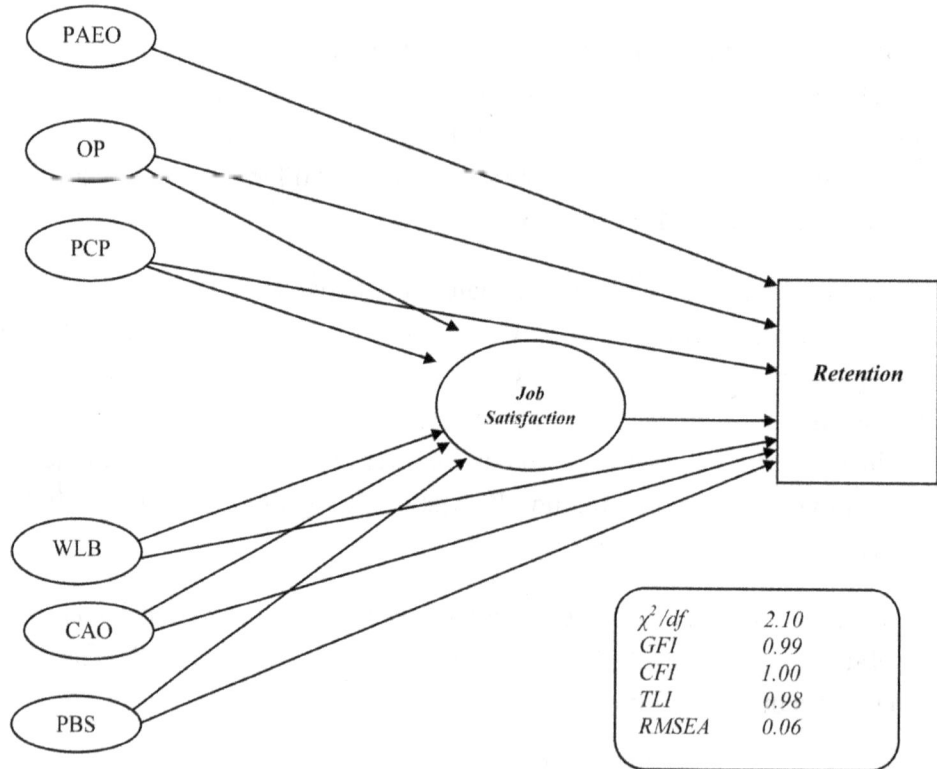

χ^2/df	2.10
GFI	0.99
CFI	1.00
TLI	0.98
RMSEA	0.06

Source: Researcher's calculations

NMIMS
Management Review
ISSN: 0971-1023
Volume XXIX
Issue-3 | July 2021

Notes: PAEO= Perceived Alternative Employment Opportunities; PCP= Perceived Competitiveness of Pay; WLB= Work-life balance; PBS= Pay and Benefits Satisfaction; CAO= Career Advancement Opportunities; OP = Organization Prestige

After assessing model fit, regression weights/path coefficients for every path between endogenous and exogenous variables and its significance was measured for the final and alternative models. Table 6 shows the squared multiple correlation *(SMC)* for each endogenous variable as well as path coefficients, t-values and standard error for each paths of final model. Path coefficient explains causal linkage between latent variables.

Table 6. Structural Model Result

Models	Endogenous & *Exogenous variables*	Path coefficient*	S.E.	t-value	Squared multiple correlations
SEM model 1 (Partial mediation)	Job Satisfaction				
	PAEO (PCP)	0.14***	0.04	3.63	
	WLB	-0.34***	0.05	-6.31	
(Re-specified model)	*PBS*	0.46***	0.06	7.39	0.70
	CAO	0.29***	0.07	4.29	
	OP	0.28***	0.04	4.80	
	Retention				
	PAEO	-0.11**	0.07	-6.59	
	WLB		0.10	7.18	
	PBS	0.17**	0.13	7.68	
	CAO	0.26**	0.13	7.44	
	OP	0.25**	0.08	13.14	0.81
	PCP	0.37**	0.09	3.54	
	JS	0.09**	0.10	0.70	
		0.05*			

Source: Researcher's calculation

Notes: PAEO= Perceived Alternative Employment Opportunities; PCP= Perceived Competitiveness of Pay; WLB= Work-life balance; PBS= Pay and Benefits Satisfaction; CAO= Career Advancement Opportunities; OP = Organization Prestige; JS = Job Satisfaction

NMIMS
NMIMS
Management Review
ISSN: 0971-1023
Volume XXIX
Issue-3 | July 2021

SE = Standard Error

standardized regression weight

*p <0.05, **p < 0.01; ***p < 0.001*

Exogenous Variables and Retention

From Table 6, PAEO was found significantly and negatively associated with retention (β = - 0.11, p< 0.01; Final SEM model). The result is consistent with the findings obtained in the aforesaid regression models. Next, work-life balance was found to have a positive and significant relation with retention of respondents (β = 0.17, p< 0.01; Final SEM model), which is uniform with regression analysis results of the current study. Pay and benefits satisfaction found to have a positive and significant relation with retention (β = 0.26, p< 0.01; Final SEM model). The result is congruous with past regression results of the current. Career advancement opportunities were found to be significant and positive in relation to retention (β = 0.25, p< 0.01; Final SEM model). This is consistent with all the regression models. A moderately investigated variable in relation to retention is organization prestige, which was analysed in the current study and found to be significantly and positively related with retention of respondents (β = 0.37, p< 0.01; Final SEM model). The result was in sync with previous findings obtained after regression. Further, PCP was found to be significantly and positively related to the retention (β = 0.09, p< 0.01; Final SEM model). A similar result was obtained in previous regression analysis. Lastly, the path between job satisfaction and retention was found significant at 0.05 level of significance in the final model of retention (β = 0.05, p< 0.05; Final SEM model) (Fig 4).

As reported in Table 6, in SEM re-specified model 1 (final model), organizational prestige had the largest effect on retention, followed by pay and benefits satisfaction, career and advancement opportunities, work-life balance, PAEO and PCP. In other words, for variance in retention length, organizational prestige has maximum contribution among all the exogenous variables and so on. Similar result was reported in the finding of regression analysis. Moreover, pay and benefits satisfaction was found to have largest effect on job satisfaction, followed by work-life balance, career advancement opportunities, organizational prestige and PAEO.

The squared multiple correlation (SMC) indicated the strength of a linear relationship. It is interpreted in the same way multiple coefficient of determination (R^2) in regression equation is interpreted. SMC is represented in Table 6 and was calculated for endogenous variables. Squared multiple correlation of 0.70 for job satisfaction and 0.91 for retention in SEM final model shows that exogenous variables in the model explains 70 percent of variance in job satisfaction and 81 percent of variance in retention.

NMIMS
Management Review
ISSN: 0971-1023
Volume XXIX
Issue-3 | July 2021

Indirect, Direct and Total Effects

To further examine the effects of exogenous variables on job satisfaction and retention, the decomposition of standardized indirect, direct and total effects of all exogenous variables on endogenous variables was conducted for each significant variable, controlling all other variables in the model (see Table 7). The direct effect of work-life balance on retention ($\beta = 0.18$, p< 0.01) was significant, the indirect effect was insignificant ($\beta = 0.00$, ns). In addition, the direct effect ($\beta = 0.24$, p< 0.01) as well as indirect effect ($\beta = 0.18$, p< 0.05) of pay and benefits satisfaction was significant on retention. The direct effect of career advancement opportunities was found to be significant with retention ($\beta = 0.24$, p< 0.01), but an insignificant indirect effect on retention ($\beta = 0.05$, ns) was reported. The direct ($\beta = 0.35$, p< 0.01) and indirect effect ($\beta = 0.01$, p < 0.05) of organizational prestige on retention was significant. Further, PCP had significant direct effect ($\beta = 0.08$, p< 0.05) and significant indirect effect on retention ($\beta = 0.01$, p< 0.05).

Table 7: Standardized Direct, Indirect and Total Effects for the final model

Endogenous & Exogenous variables	Direct effect	Indirect effect	Total effect
Retention			
PAEO	-0.114**	-	- 0.114**
WLB	0.183**	-0.006	0.177**
PBS	0.245**	0.018*	0.263**
CAO	0.249**	0.005	0.251**
OP	0.355**	0.015*	0.370**
PCP	0.089*	0.010*	0.099**
JS	0.051*	-	0.051*

Source: Researcher's calculation

Notes: PAEO= Perceived Alternative Employment Opportunities; PCP= Perceived Competitiveness of Pay; WLB= Work-life balance; PBS= Pay and Benefits Satisfaction; CAO= Career Advancement Opportunities; OP = Organization Prestige; JS = Job Satisfaction

*$p < 0.05$; ** $p < 0.01$; *** $p < 0.001$

6. Discussion and Implications

The study contributes to the existing literature on employee retention. The purpose of the study was to identify the variables influencing the retention of managers in private banks and proposing an initial model and two alternative models using those variables, which were validated using empirical data from the selected Indian private

NMIMS
SVKM'S
Deemed to be UNIVERSITY

NMIMS
Management Review
ISSN: 0971-1023
Volume XXIX
Issue-3 | July 2021

bank managers. The initial model propounded had job satisfaction as mediator and since not all the endogenous variables included in the current study had been examined in relation to job satisfaction as mediator and retention as the exogenous variable in the past, individual literature on employee retention and job satisfaction was used to create linkage between the selected endogenous factors, job satisfaction and retention of managers. It should be noted that our main hypothesized model was rejected in favour of a model that contained, in addition to the predicted paths, a path between organizational prestige and job satisfaction. The addition of this path gave the best model fit model among all the three SEM models and was accepted as the final model.

Multiple and hierarchical regression analysis was conducted to the selected determinants of retention and nine significant determinants identified after regression was used to create a SEM model. When SEM models were tested, the best fit model gave a similar result with regression analysis. Therefore, result in SEM as well as regression showed that PAEO is directly and negatively related to employee retention, which is consistent with previous researches (e.g., Huang et al.,2006). Thus, when managers do not perceive a number of suitable/better alternative opportunities outside in the market then the mangers stay. Organizational prestige is the most important indicator of employee retention. The regression as well as SEM models has a direct and positive impact on employee retention, and has the second highest indirect impact through job satisfaction. Although not been studied much organizational prestige has shown remarkable results in relation to employee retention. The positive influence of organizational prestige on retention is in sync with previous studies (e.g., Hausknecht et al.,2009; Xu, 2008) and implies that when employees feel that organization has a countable image in the external environment, it not only makes them stay but make them more satisfied and proud with their job, which then increases retention for them. PBS, with the highest and positive impact on employee retention after organizational prestige, it was found to have a direct as well as the strongest indirect effect on employee retention through job satisfaction. This indicates that being positive about pay and benefits provided by the firm, directly enhances the retention of managers in the bank. The result is consent with (Price & Mueller, 1981). Also, PBS influences job satisfaction positively and increased employee retention. The presence of a similar indirect path was supported by Buchko (1992) and Shaw et al. (1998),claims that higher pay and better fringe benefits positively influence the employee's decision to stay on the job, as it increases job satisfaction.

CAO being the third vital determinant of retention showed second highest direct effect but the indirect effect was not significant. Therefore, with the perception of career opportunities in the firm for further growth, retention is seen in managers, which is consistent with past studies (Daniels et al.,2007). Whereas, the literature shows the impact of advancement opportunities on job satisfaction (Zeitz, 1990) and

NMIMS
Management Review
ISSN: 0971-1023
Volume XXIX
Issue-3 | July 2021

job satisfaction on retention but the study could not prove job satisfaction to mediate the relation between CAO and retention of managers. On the other hand, WLB is the fourth prominent indicator of employee retention in the study, with no indirect but a significant direct and positive effect on the retention of managers. Thus, it can be stated that by being able to maintain balance in work and life, the managers stay longer. Similar findings were reported by previous studies such as George (2015). However, in an environment, if one is not being able to maintain a balance between work and life that will probably make them leave, without even considering their satisfaction with the job. PCP was found to have an impact on retention. Although the coefficient for PCP is the second smallest but it indicated a significant and positive relation between PCP and retention. In addition to that, a significant direct and indirect effect of PCP on retention was noticed. This indicates that not only perception of fair pay makes an employee stay, but it shows a significant and positive impact on job satisfaction, which later increases the retention of managers. Among the three exogenous variables were found to have a significant indirect effect on retention through job satisfaction, two of them are PCP and PBS. The result of these two pay-related variables affecting retention through job satisfaction is in consistence with the literature, as pay related satisfaction is a part of the larger job satisfaction construct (Pitts, Marvel& Fernandez, 2011) and hence is expected to have an influence on job satisfaction (Price & Mueller 1981) The findings of the present study can be theorized based on equity theory of motivation, which suggests that individuals are motivated when offered fair or equal treatment with other employees. If an employee feels the pay and benefits given to them are fair in relation to what others are availing in and outside the organization, for a similar job will feel that they are equally treated and therefore are motivated to stay. While the literature calls pay-related variables as 'modest predictors' (Griffethet al., 2000), this was not the case in this study. In SEM model, job satisfaction was found to be significantly and positively related to retention but with the smallest coefficient value. This refers that an increase in job satisfaction enhances retention of managers but the relation is highly moderate.

A majority of the models in literature are focused on employee turnover (such as Lee & Mitchell, 1994; Steers & Mowday, 1981), whereas the past researchers have argued that the reasons of retention and turnover for individuals are not opposite (Reitz & Anderson, 2011) or same (Steel et al., 2002). Employee turnover and retention are not two sides of the same construct. In response to the argument of the past studies, the study contributes a retention model for this line of research, which is entirely focused on determinants of retention. It should be noticed that rather than creating and testing 1 theoretical model, alternative SEM models were proposed and tested in the study to include the maximum possible variety of relation between the predictor and outcome variables. And, the final model of the study found to have the best fit that did not lead to any differences in the primary result of relation

NMIMS
NMIMS
Management Review
ISSN: 0971-1023
Volume XXIX
Issue-3 | July 2021

between variables, which further authenticate the findings. Another contribution of the study is the segmentation of total effects into direct and indirect effects of predictor variables.

Adding to previous work in this area, results highlight the importance of some of the conventional variables on employee retention, viz. pay satisfaction related variables, work-life balance and career advancement opportunities. Contrary to the past, two of the most hopeful variables to have a significant impact on retention, could not be much effective, viz. job satisfaction and organizational commitment, whereas one of the unused variables, viz. organizational prestige proved to be most significantly related to employee retention.

In response to Shore and Martin (1989) recommendations, professionals have different reason than non-professional to stay, the present work focused only on professional employees. Also, unlike many other studies (e.g.,Allen & Shanock, 2013) focusing on 1 or 2 variables, the study has an exhaustive and partially exclusive list of variables studied in relation to employee retention.

Using stratified random sampling the study made sure to include samples from various regions of Delhi, which may mitigate concern about the generalizability of findings in the concerned industry.

In the presence of abundant studies on retention or turnover and their determinants, there are moderate number of studies on retention model and no universally accepted determinants, therefore a retention model or any new information regarding the same will be relevant for managerial practices.

The authority could utilize the findings of the study to retain talents in the organization. Based on the result, the organizations should be highly considerate about their image in the society, if they are worried about retention. Apart from that, the study indicates that the banks should focus on decent perks, help to get the employees a balance between work and life and opportunities for career development.

As individual variables of the respondents were found to affect manager's retention, banks can take it as a lesson and should keep it in thought while framing retention policies for the organization.

REFERENCES

Abelson, M.A. (1987). Examination of Avoidable and Unavoidable Turnover. *Journal of Applied Psychology*, 72, 382-386.

Abelson, M.A. & Baysinger, B.D. (1984). Optimal and Dysfunctional Turnover: Toward an Organizational Level Model. *Academy of Management Journal*, 9, 331-141.

Ahmad, N., Iqbal, N. & Sheeraz, M. (2012). The Effect of Internal Marketing on Employee Retention in Pakistani Banks. *International Journal of Academic Research in Business and Social Sciences*, 2 (8), 270-280.

Allen, D.G., Shore, L.M. & Griffeth R.W. (2003). The Role of Perceived Organizational Support and Supportive Human Resource Practices in the Turnover Process. *Journal of Management*, 29 (1), 99-118.

Allen, D.G., Bryant, P.C. & Vardaman, J.M. (2010). Retaining talent: Replacing misconceptions with evidence-based strategies. *Academy of Management Perspectives*, 24, 48–65. doi:10.5465/AMP .2010.51827775

Allen, D.G. & Shanock, L.R. (2013). Perceived Organizational Support and Embeddedness as Key Mechanisms Connecting Socialization Tactics to Commitment and Turnover among New Employees. *Journal of Organizational Behaviour*, 34, 350-369.

Ariff, M. (1988). A Behavioural Proxy Model for Employee Turnover: Results from a Singapore study. *Asia Pacific Journal of Management*, 5 (3), 197-206.

Armstrong-Stassen, M. & Cameron, S.J. (2005). Concerns, Satisfaction, and Retention of Canadian Community Health Nurses. *Journal of Community Health Nursing*, 22 (4), 181-194.

Babbie, E. (2007). *The Practice of Social Research* (Eleventh edition). Wadsworth, Belmont, CA: Cencage Learning.

Bambacas, M. & Kulik, C.T. (2012). Job Embeddedness in China: How HR practices Impact Turnover Intentions. *The International Journal of Human Resource Management*, 1–20, iFirst, DOI:10.1080/09585192.2012.725074.

Barkman, A.I., Sheridan, J.E. & Peters, L.H. (1992). Survival Models of Professional Staff Retention in Public Accounting Firms. *Journal of Managerial Issues*, 4 (3), 339-353.

Bassi, L.J. & Van Buren, M.E. (1999). Sharpening the Leading Edge. *Training & Development*, 53, 23-32.

Batt, R. & Valcour, P.M. (2003). Human Resources Practices as Predictors of Work–Family Outcomes and Employee Turnover. *Industrial Relations*, 42,189–220.

Bhatnagar, J. (2012). Management of Innovation: Role of Psychological Empowerment, Work engagement and Turnover Intention in the Indian context. *The International Journal of Human Resource Management*, 23 (5), 928-951.

Birdseye, M.G. & Hill, J.S. (1995). Individual, Organizational/Work and Environmental Influences on Expatriate Turnover Tendencies: An Empirical Study. *Journal of InternationalBusiness Studies*, 26 (4), 787-813.

Bluedorn, A.C. (1982). A Unified Model of Turnover from Organizations. *Human Relations*, 35(2), 135-153.

NMIMS
NMIMS
Management Review
ISSN: 0971-1023
Volume XXIX
Issue-3 | July 2021

Branham, L. (2006). *The 7 Hidden Reasons Employees Leave: How to recognize the subtle signs and act before it's too late*. New York, NY: AMACOM.

Brereton, D., Beach, R. & Cliff, D. (2003). Employee Turnover as a Sustainability Issue'. Paper presented at *Mineral Council of Australia's 2003 Sustainable Development Conference*. Brisbane, Australia, Available From: http://www.csrm.uq.edu.au/docs/MCApaperTurnover1.pdf

Buchko, A.A. (1992). Employee Ownership, Attitudes, and Turnover: An Empirical Assessment. *Human Relations*, 45(7), 711-33.

Byrne, B.M. (2001). *Structural Equation Modeling with AMOS: Basic Concepts, Applications and Programming*. Mahwah, NJ: Lawrence Erlbaum Associates.

Cardy, R.L. & Lengnick-Hall, M.L. (2011). Will They Stay or Will They Go? Exploring a Customer-Oriented Approach to Employee Retention. *J Bus Psychol*, 26, 213-217.

Cohen, A. & Golan, R. (2007). Predicting Absenteeism and Turnover Intentions by Past Absenteeism and Work Attitudes: An Empirical Examination of Female Employees in Long Term Nursing Care Facilities. *Career Development International*, 12(5), 416–432.

Cortina, J. (1993) What is Coefficient Alpha? An Examination of Theory and Applications. *Journal of Applied Psychology*, 78 (1), 98–104.

Cotton, J.L. &Tuttle, J.M. (1986). Employee Turnover: A Meta-Analysis and Review with Implication for Research. *The Academy of Management Review*, 11(1), 55-70.

Daniels, Z.M., VanLeit, B.J., Skipper, B.J., Sanders, M.L. & Rhyne, R.L. (2007). Factors in Recruiting and Retaining Health Professionals for Rural Practice. *National Rural Health Association*, 23(1), 62-71.

Dess, G.G. and Shaw, J.D. (2001). Voluntary Turnover Social Capital and Organizational Performance. *Academy of Management Review*, 26 (3), 446-456.

Dickinson, N.S. & Perry, R.E. (2002). Factors Influencing the Retention of Specially Educated Public Child Welfare Workers. *Evaluation Research in Child Welfare*, 15(3/4), 89–103.

Dogan, H. (2008). A Research Study for Procedural Justice as a Factor in Employee Retention. *Yonetim ve Ekononomi*, 15(2),61-71.

Dries, N. (2013). The Psychology of Talent Management: A Review and Research Agenda, *Human Resource Management Review*, 23 (4), 272-285.

Duncan, C., & Loretto, W. (2004). Never the right age? Gender and age☐based discrimination in employment. *Gender, Work & Organization*, 11(1), 95-115.

Ellenbecker, C.H. (2004). A Theoretical Model of Job Retention for Home Health Care Nurses. *Journal of Advanced Nursing*, 47(3), 303-310.

Ewalt, P.L. (1991). Trends Affecting Recruitment and Retention of Social Work Staff in Human Services Agencies. *Oxford Journals*, 36(3), 214-217.

NMIMS
Management Review
ISSN: 0971-1023
Volume XXIX
Issue-3 | July 2021

Farrell, D. & Rusbult, C.E. (1981). Exchange Variables as Predictors of Job Satisfaction, Job Commitment and Turnover: The Impact of Rewards, Costs, Alternative and Investments. *Organizational Behavior and Human Performance*, 27, 172-186.

Finegold, D., Mohrman, S., & Spreitzer, G.M. (2002). Age Effects on the Predictors of Technical Workers' Commitment and Willingness to Turnover. *Journal of Organizational Behavior*, 23,655–674.

Flowers, V.S. & Hughes, C.L. (1973). Why Employees Stay. *Harvard Business Review*, 51(4), 49-60.

Frenkel, S., Sanders, K. & Bednall, T. (2012). Employee Perceptions of Management Relations as Influences on Job Satisfaction and Quit Intentions. *Asia Pac J Manag.* DOI 10.1007/s10490-012-9290-z

Friedlander, F. (1964). Job characteristics as Satisfiers and Dissatisfiers. *Journal of Applied Psychology*, 48 (6), 388-392.

Gaertner, K.H. & Nollen, S.D. (1992). Turnover Intentions and Desire among Executives. *Human Relations*, Working paper 08-06, 1-34.

George, C. (2015). Retaining Professional Workers: What makes them Stay? *Employee Relations,* 37(1), 102 – 121.

Gerhart, B. (1990). Voluntary Turnover and Alternative Job Opportunities. *Journal of AppliedPsychology,* 95(5), 467-476.

Ghosh, P., Satyawadi, R., Joshi, J.P. & Shadman, Mohd (2013). Who Stays With You? Factors Predicting Employees' Intention to Stay. *International Journal of Organizational Analysis*, 21(3), 288 – 312.

Gorsuch, R.L. (2003). Factor Analysis. InJ.A. Schinka & W. F. Velicer (Eds.), *Handbook of psychology*: *Research methods in psychology* (2,143-164),Hoboken, NJ: John Wiley.

Govaerts, N., Kyndt, E., Dochy, F. & Baert, H. (2011). Influence of Learning and Working Climate on the Retention of Talented Employees. *Journal of Workplace Learning*, 23(1), 35 – 55.

Griffeth, R.W., Hom, P.W. & Gaertner, S. (2000). A Meta-Analysis of Antecedents and Correlates of Employee Turnover: Update, Moderator Tests, and Research Implications for the Next Millennium. *Journal of Management*, 26, 463-488.

Griffeth, R.W. & Hom, P.W. (2001). *Retaining Valued Employees*, Thousand Oaks, CA: Sage Publications.

Gupta, S. (2011). *Retention of managers in IT Sector: A Case Study.* PhD Thesis. Veer Bahadur Singh Purvanchal University.

Gurunathan, K.B. & Vijayalakshmi, V. (2012). Theoretical Construct on Employee Retention Strategies and Its Bang in Automobile Industry in India. *European Journal of Social Science*, 34(2), 254-262.

NMIMS
Management Review
ISSN: 0971-1023
Volume XXIX
Issue-3 | July 2021

Hausknecht, J., Rodda, J.M. & Howard, M.J. (2008). Targeted Employee Retention: Performance-Based and Related Differences in Reported Reasons for Staying. *Centre for Advanced Human Resource Studies,* Working paper 08-06, 1-34.

Hausknecht, J.P., Charlie, O.T. & Michael J.H. (2009). Unit Level Voluntary Turnover Rates and Customer Service Quality: Implications of Group Cohesiveness, Newcomer Concentration and Size. *Journal of Applied Psychology*, 94 (4), 1068-1075.

Hom, P., Leong, F., & Golubovich, J. (2010). Insights from vocational and career developmental theories: Their potential contributions for advancing the understanding of employee turnover. In H. Liao, J. Martocchio, & A. Joshi (Eds.), *Research in personnel and human resources management* (29, pp. 115–166). Bingley, England: Emerald Group.

Huang, I.C., Lin, H.C. & Chuang, C.H. (2006). Constructing Factors Related to Worker Retention. *International Journal of Manpower,* 27 (5), 491 – 508.

Hulin, C.L., Roznowski, M. & Hachiya, D. (1985). Alternative Opportunities and Withdrawal Decisions: Empirical and Theoretical Discrepancies and an Integration. *Psychology Bulletin*, 97, 233-250.

Ibarra, H. & Barbulescu, R. (2010). Identity as narrative: Prevalence, effectiveness, and consequences of narrative identity work in macro work role transitions. *Academy of Management Journal*, 35, 135-154.

Idson, T.L. & Valletta, R.G. (1996). Seniority, Sectoral Decline, and Employee Retention: An Analysis of Layoff Unemployment Spells. *Journal of Labor Economics*, 14, 654-76.

Jayakumar, U.M. Howard, T.C., Allen, W.R. & Han, J.C. (2009). Racial Privilege in the Professoriate: An Exploration of Campus Climate, Retention, and Satisfaction. *The Journal of Higher Education,* 80 (5), 538-563.

Jayaratne, S. & Chess, W.A. (1984). Factors associated with Job Satisfaction and Turnover among Child Welfare Workers. In J. Laird and A. Hartmann (Eds.), *A Handbook of Child Welfare: Context, Knowledge, and Practice* (pp. 760–766). New York: Free Press.

Joseph, K. & Kalwani, M.U. (1992). Do Bonus Payments Help Enhance Salesforce Retention? *Marketing Letters*, 3 (4), 331-341.

Kanwar, Y.P.S., Singh, A.K. & Kodwani, A.D. (2012). A Study of Job Satisfaction, Organizational Commitment and Turnover Intent among the IT and ITES Sector Employees. *Vision*, 16 (1), 27-35.

Khatri, M., Budhwar, P. & Fern, C.T. (n.d.). Employee Turnover: Bad Attitude or Poor Management. Available from: http://citeseerx.ist.psu.edu/viewdoc/download?doi=10.1.1.56 9.4082&rep=rep1&type=pdf

Khatri, N., Fern, C. T., & Budhwar, P. (2001). Explaining employee turnover in an Asian context. *Human Resource Management Journal*, 11(1), 54.

Knight, W.E. & Leimer, C.L. (2010). Will IR Staff Stick? An Exploration of Institutional Researchers' Intention to Remain in or Leave their Jobs. *Research in Higher Education,* 51 (2), 109-131.

Kumar, R. & Arora, R. (2012). Determinants of Talent Retention in BPO industry. *The Indian Journal of Industrial Relations*, 48 (2), 259-273.

Kyndt, E., Dochy, F., Michielsen, M. & Moeyaert, B. (2009). Employee Retention: Organizational and Personal Perspectives. *Vocations and Learning*, 2 (3), 195-215.

Latour, S.A. & Peat, N.C. (1979). Conceptual and Methodological Issues in Consumer Satisfaction Research. In W. L. Wilkie (Ed.), *Advances in Consumer Research* (pp. 431- 437). Ann Arbor, MI: Association for Consumer Research.

Lee, C.H. & Bruvold, N.T. (2003). Creating Value for Employees: Investment in Employee Development. *Int. J. of Human Resource Management,* 14 (6), 981-1000.

Lee, T.W. & Mitchell, T.R. (1994). An Alternative Approach: The Unfolding Model of Employee Turnover. *Academy of Management Review*, 91 (1), 51-89.

Lee, T.W. & Maurer, S. (1999). The Effects of Family Structure on Organizational Commitment, Intention to Leave, and Voluntary Turnover. *Journal of Managerial Issues*, 11(4), 493-513.

Liu, Z., Cai, Z., Li, J., Shi, S. & Fang, Y. (2013). Leadership Style and Employee Turnover Intentions: A Social Identity Perspective. *Career Development International*, 18 (3), 305 – 324,

Lyness, K.S. & Judiesch, M.K. (2001). Are Female Managers Quitters? The Relationships of gender, promotions, and family leaves of absence on turnover. *Journal of Applied Psychology*, 86,1167-1178.

MacManus, S.A. & Strunz, K.C. (1993). Employee Surveys as a Strategic Management Tool: The Case of Army Physician Retention. *Public Administration Quarterly*, 17(2), 175-200.

Maertz, C.P. & Campion, M.A. (1998). 25 years of Voluntary Turnover Research: A Review and Critique. In CL Cooper and IT Robertson (Eds.), *International Review of Industrial and Organizational Psychology* (13, 49-81). New York, NY: Wiley.

March, J.G. & Simon, H.A. (1958). *Organizations,* New York: John Wiley.

Marsh, H.W., Balla, J.R. & McDonald, R.P. (1988). Goodness-Of-Fit Indexes in Confirmatory Factor Analysis: The Effect of Sample Size. *Psychological Bulletin*, 103, 391-410.

Martin, T.N. (1979). A Contextual Model of Employee Turnover Intentions. *The Academy of Management Journal*, 22 (2), 313-324.

McBey, K. & Karakowsky, L. (2001). Examining Sources of Influence on Employee Turnover in the Part-Time Work Context. *Career Development International*, 6 (1), 39 – 48.

NMIMS
SVKM'S
Deemed to be UNIVERSITY

NMIMS
Management Review
ISSN: 0971-1023
Volume XXIX
Issue-3 | July 2021

Milman, A. & Dickson, D. (2014). Employment Characteristics and Retention Predictors among Hourly Employees in Large US Theme Parks and Attractions. *International Journal of Contemporary Hospitality Management*, 26 (3), 447 – 469.

Min, H. (2007). Examining Sources of Warehouse Employee Turnover. *International Journal of Physical Distribution & Logistics Management*, 37 (5), 375 – 388.

Mitchell, O., Mackenzie, D.L., Styve, G.J. & Gover, A.R. (2000). The impact of individual, organizational, and environmental attributes on voluntary turnover among juvenile correctional staff members. *Justice Quarterly*, 17 (2), 333-357.

Mitchell, T.R., Holtom, B.C., Lee, T.W., Sablynski, C.J. & Erez, M. (2001). Why People Stay: Using Job Embeddedness to Predict Voluntary Turnover. *The Academy of Management Journal*, 44 (6),1102–1121.

Mobley, W.H., Griffeth, R.W., Hand, H.H. & Meglino, B.M. (1979). Review and Conceptual Analysis of the Employee Turnover Process. *Psychological Bulletin*, 86, 493-522.

Mowday, R.T., Steers R.M. & Porter L.W. (1979). The Measurement of Organizational Commitment. *Journal of Vocational Behavior*, 14, 224–247.

Mumford, K. & Smith, P.N. (2004). Job Tenure in Britain: Employee Characteristics versus Workplace Effects. *Economica*, 71 (282), 275-298.

Neter, J., Wasserman, W., & Kutner, M.H. (1989). *Applied Linear Regression Models*. Homewood, IL: Richard D Irwin Inc.

Oliver, R.L. (1980). A Cognitive Model of the Antecedents and Consequences of Satisfaction Decisions. *Journal of Marketing Research*, 17, 460-469.

Palomino, P.R., Canas, R.M. & Fontrodona, J. (2013). Ethical Culture and Employee Outcomes: The Mediating Role of Person-Organization Fit. *J Bus Ethics*, 116, 173-188.

Parmar, B. (2015). With New Players in Fray, Private Banks Face Talent Poaching Threat. *The Hindu-Business Line*, Available from: http://www.thehindubusinessline.com/money-and-banking/with-new-players-in-fray-private-banks-face-talent-poaching-threat/article7659983.ece

Pitts, D., Marvel, J. & Fernandez, S. (2011). So Hard to Say Goodbye? Turnover Intention among U.S. Federal Employees. *Public Administration Review*, September|October, 751-760.

Porter, L.W. & Steers, R.M. (1973). Organizational, Work, and Personal Factors in Employee Turnover and Absenteeism. *Psychological Bulletin*, 80, 151-176.

Porter, L.W., Steers, R.M., Mowday, R.T. & Boulian, P.V. (1974). Organizational Commitment, Job Satisfaction and Turnover among Psychiatric Technicians. *Journal of Applied Psychology*, 59, 603-609.

Price, J.L. & Mueller, C.W. (1981). A Causal Model of Turnover for Nurses. *Academy of Management Journal*, 24 (3), 543-565.

Price, J.L. & Mueller, C.W. (1986). Absenteeism *and Turnover of Hospital Employees*, JAI Press Inc.

Rahman, W. & Nas, Z. (2013). Employee *Development and Turnover Intention: Theory Validation. European Journal of Training and Development*, 37 (6), 564 – 579.

Reitz, O.E. & Anderson, M.A. (2011). An Overview of Job Embeddedness. *Journal of Professional Nursing: Official Journal of the American Association of College of Nursing*, 27 (5), 320-327.

Rentsch, J.R. & Steel, R.P. (1998). Testing the Durability of Job Characteristics as Predictors of Absenteeism over a Six-Year Period. *Personnel Psychology*, 51, 165-190.

Richardson, H. (1994). Can We Afford the Driver Shortage? *Transportation and Distribution*, 35 (8), 30-33.

Riordan, C.M. & Griffeth, R.W. (1995). The Opportunity for Friendship in the Workplace: An Underexplored Construct, *Journal of Business and Psychology*, 10 (2), 141-154.

Rycraft, J.R. (1994). The Party Isn't Over: The Agency Role in the Retention of Public Child Welfare Caseworkers. *Social Work*, 39 (1), 75-80.

Sahu, A. & Gupta, M. (1999). An Empirical Analysis of Employee Turnover in a Software Organization. *Shri Ram Centre for Industrial Relations and Human Resources*, 35 (1), 55-73.

Sengupta, S. & Gupta, A. (2012). Exploring the Dimensions of Attrition in Indian BPOs. *The International Journal of Human Resource Management*, 23 (6),1259-1288

Setia, M. & Singh, D. (2014). Employee retention: A challenge faced by Indian banking industry-A study. *International Journal of Current Research*, 6 (11), 9856-9860.

Shaw, J., Delery, J., Jenkins, G. Jr & Gupta, N. (1998). An Organization-Level Analysis of Voluntary and Involuntary Turnover. *Academy of Management Journal,* 41 (5), 511-26.

Shore, L.F. & Martin, H.J. (1989). Job Satisfaction and Organizational Commitment in Relation to Work Performance and Turnover Intentions. *Human Relations*, 72 (7), 625-638.

Shrivastava, P. & Bhatnagar, J. (2012). Employer Brand for Talent Acquisition: An Analysis towards its Measurement. *Vision- The Journal of Business Perspective*, 14 (1 & 2), 25-34.

Sightler, K.W. & Adams, J.S. (1999). Difference between Stayers and Leavers among Part-Time Workers. *Journal of Managerial Issues*, 11 (1), 110-125.

Steers, R. & Mowday, R. (1981). Employee Turnover and Postdecision Accommodation Processes. In L. Cumming, & B. Staw (Eds.), *Research in Organizational Behavior.* Greenwich, CI: JAI Press.

Steel, R.P., Griffeth, R.W. & Hom, P.W. (2002). Practical Retention Policy for the Practical Manager. *Academy of Management Executive*, 16 (2), 149-162.

Steers, R.M. (1977). Antecedents and Outcomes of Organizational Commitment. *Administrative Science Quarterly*, 22, 46-56.

Stumpf, S.A. & Dawley, P.K. (1981). Predicting Voluntary Turnover and Involuntary Turnover Using Absenteeism and Performance Indicies. *Academy of Management Journal*, 24, 148-163.

Tanwar, K. & Prasad, A. (2016). Exploring a Relationship between Employer Branding and Employee Retention. Global Research Review, 17(3S), 1S–21S.

Taylor, G.S., Garver, M.S. & Williams, Z. (2010). Owner Operators: Employing a Segmentation Approach to Improve Retention. *The International Journal of Logistics Management*, 21 (2), 207 – 229.

Taylor, L.J., III, Murphy, B. & Price, W. (2006). Goldratt's Thinking Process Applied to Employee Retention. *Business Process Management Journal*, 12 (5), 646 – 670.

Terborg, J.R. & Lee, T.W. (1984). A Predictive Study of Organizational Turnover Rates. *Academy of Management Journal*, 27, 793-810.

Thatcher, J.B., Stepina, L.P. & Boyle, R.J. (2002-03). Turnover of Information Technology Workers: Examining Empirically the Influence of Attitudes Job Characteristics, And External Markets, *Journal of Management Information Systems,* 19 (3), 231-261.

Thite, M. & Rusell, B. (2010). Work Organization, Human Resource Practices and Employee Retention in Indian Call Centers. *Asia Pacific Journal of Human Resource,* 48 (3), 356-374.

Thompson, K.R. & Terpening, W.D. (1983). Job-Type Variations and Antecedents to Intention to Leave: A content approach to turnover. *Human Relations,* 36, 655-682.

Van Hamme, S. (2009). *Talent Development for employees: The Relationship Between the Learning Environment and Retention,* Master thesis, University of Leuven.

Vandenberg, R.J. & Nelson, J.B. (1999). Disaggregating the Motives Underlying Turnover Intentions: Why do Intentions Predict Turnover Behaviour? *Human Relations,* 152 (10), 1313-1336.

Vegt, G.S., Bunderson, S. & Kuipers, B. (2010). Why Turnover Matters in a Self-Managing Workteams: Leaning Social Integration and Task Flexibility. *Journal of Management,* 36 (5), 1168-1191.

Vispute, S. (2013). Recruitment Strategy and Employee Retention in India Banking and Insurance Sector. *International Journal of Arts & Sciences,* 6 (2), 743-756.

Volkwein, J. F. (1999). The Four Faces of Institutional Research. In JF Volkwein(Ed.), *What is Institutional Research all about? A Critical and Comprehensive Assessment of the Profession* (104, pp. 9-19). San Francisco: Jossey-Bass.

Vos, A.D. and Meganck, A. (2007). What HR Managers do versus what Employees Value:

Exploring Both Parties' views on Retention Management from a Psychological Contract Perspective. *Personnel Review*, 38 (1), 45-60.

Webb, M.C. & Carpenter, J. (2012). What Can Be Done to Promote the Retention of Social Workers? A Systematic Review of Interventions. *British Journal of Social Work*, 42, 1245-1255. DOI:10.1093/bjsw/bcr144.

Xu, Y.J. (2008). Gender Disparity in STEM Disciplines: A Study of Faculty Attrition and Turnover Intentions. *Research in Higher Education*, 49 (7), 607-624.

Yamamoto, H. (2013). The Relationship Between Employees' Perceptions of Human Resource Management and Their Retention: From the Viewpoint of Attitudes Toward Job Specialties. *The International Journal of Human Resource Management*, 24 (4), 747-767.

Yang, S.B. & Lee, K.M. (2009). Linking Empowerment and Job Enrichment to Turnover Intention: The Influence of Job Satisfaction. *International Review of Public Administration*, 14 (2), 13-23.

Zeitz, G. (1990). Age and Work Satisfaction in a Government Agency: A Situational Perspective. *Human Relations*, 43 (5), 419–438.

Zhou, Y. & Volkwein, J.F. (2004). Examining the Influences on Faculty Departure Intentions: A Comparison of Tenured Versus Non-Tenured Faculty at Research Universities Using NSOPF-99. *Research in Higher Education*, 45 (2), 139-176.

Niharika Singh is Assistant Professor at ICFAI University Tripura and can be reached at niharika240388@gmail.com. His ORCID id is https://orcid.org/0000-0001-8577-9874

L. Shashikumar Sharma is Professor at Mizoram University and can be reached at lsksharma@yahoo.co.in. His ORCID id is https://orcid.org/0000-0002-9040-6033

Dr Bendangienla Aier is a Post Doctoral Fellow under RUSA 2.0 at Centre of Excellence; Unorganised Labour, Utkal University, Bhubaneswar, Odisha. She can be reached at abendangienla@yahoo.com. His ORCID id is https://orcid.org/0000-0001-7961-2664

NMIMS

NMIMS
Management Review
ISSN: 0971-1023
Volume XXIX
Issue-3 | July 2021

Does Work-Life Balance Mediate the Relationship of Perceived Organizational Support and Job Satisfaction for Healthcare Workers? A Study on Female Nurses in India

Received: 17 April 2021
Revised: 12 June 2021
Accepted: 4 Sept 2021

https://doi.org/10.53908/NMMR.290304

Arunkumar Dubey • S. Riasudeen

Abstract

Purpose: Studies time and again ascribe increased attrition in the nursing profession to poor organizational support and issues of work-life balance resulting in higher levels of job dissatisfaction among nurses. Considering this background, we conceptualized a model (POS-WLB-JS) anchored on organizational support theory and examined the mediating influence of work-life balance in the relationship of perceived organizational support and job satisfaction for female nurses in the Indian healthcare ecosystem.

Methodology: Convenience sampling techniques were used to collect data from 250 female nurses from 40 hospitals in Mumbai. Hierarchical regression analysis techniques were used to test the hypotheses. In addition, Sobel test for indirect effects was used to assess the mediating influence of work-life balance in the conceptual model.

Findings: Perceived organizational support, work-life balance, and job satisfaction have a significant and positive relationship among them. In addition, work-life balance mediates the relationship of perceived organizational support and job satisfaction for female nurses in the Indian nursing context.

Practical Implications: The study will be beneficial to healthcare administrators, doctors, and practitioners who play a pivotal role in the delivery of healthcare services through nurses. It explores the process of job satisfaction through work-life balance and organizational support.

Originality: The study makes a distinction between specific support for work-life measures and distal support that exists for nurses in hospitals. It was found that the latter as measured by the perceived organizational support scale has a significant and positive relationship with job satisfaction and work-life balance.

Keywords: *Perceived Organizational Support, Work-life Balance, Job Satisfaction, Healthcare, Female Nurses.*

NMIMS
Management Review
ISSN: 0971-1023
Volume XXIX
Issue-3 | July 2021

1. Introduction

Nursing remains one of the preferred jobs for many women in India (Johnson, Judith, & Maben, 2014). They represent the largest front-line workforce in the entire healthcare ecosystem. The number of nurses working in urban areas is almost thrice than those employed in rural areas as nurses prefer working in cities (Gill, 2011; Park, 2011). However, of late, nursing as a profession is losing its charm given a plethora of challenges and concerns associated with it. FICCI (2016) in its report identified some of the pressing concerns in the nursing profession such as lack of rewarding career progression, poor welfare measures, income disparity, low social status, inadequate work environment, poor work life balance , and issues of empowerment. Furthermore, regular nursing tasks are physically and emotionally challenging (Demerouti, Bakker, & Bulters, 2004; McQueen, 2004) contributing to a higher level of stress in nurses. Therefore, job satisfaction (JS) for clinically focused nurses is considered as one of the main factors affecting their recruitment and retention, contributing to nurses shortages and staff turnover, which are issues of both national as well as international concern (Kumar, Dass, & Topaloglu, 2014; Alotaibi, Paliadelis, & Valenzuela, 2016).

Importantly, low job satisfaction impacts the quality of patient care (Cavanagh, 1992) and in turn the reputation of hospitals (Poulose& Sudarsan, 2017). Furthermore, studies on the satisfaction of nurses in metropolitan cities have revealed the prevalence of huge dissatisfaction among the nurses on almost all satisfaction rating scales (Murray and Smith, 1988, Kuaru, 1994). The problems caused due to such dissatisfaction leads to absenteeism, grievances, low morale, and high turnover (Gangadhraiah, Nardev, & Reddy, 1990; Martin, 1990 & Abou Hashish, 2017). Han, Carter, and Champion (2018) in a study on job satisfaction of nurses found that a greater portion of job dis-satisfiers was extrinsic including company policies, working conditions, and compensation. Such dissatisfaction results in the poor perception of organizational support by the nurses. (Aiken, Clarke, Sloane, Sochalski, & Silber, 2002; Kwak, Chung, Xu, & Cho, 2010).

According to Organizational Support Theory (OST), employees develop a general perception of support for their organizations' approach in terms of caring for their contribution and well-being which is referred to as perceived organizational support (POS) (Eisenberger, Huntington, Hutchison, & Sowa, 1986; Shore & Shore, 1995; Eisenberger & Stinglhamber, 2011). Studies on POS are in abundance and have explained time and again the significance of it in predicting job satisfaction in the nursing context too (for reference see, Li et al., 2020; Gillet et al., 2013 &Chang, 2015). However, studies linking such distal support (general support) to work-life balance in the healthcare settings are limited (McCarthy et al., 2013; Amazue & Onyishi, 2016). Furthermore, explicit work-life balance measures may or may not exist for nurses considering the very demanding nature of their work in the healthcare sector.

NMIMS

NMIMS Management Review
ISSN: 0971-1023
Volume XXIX
Issue-3 | July 2021

Thus, we argue, even distal perception of organizational support as conceptualized in terms of perceived organizational support too would promote work life balance and job satisfaction. Therefore, anchoring our research on organizational support theory, we proposed a theoretical model and examined the effect of perceived organizational support on job satisfaction through the mediating influence of work-life balance for female nurses in the Indian healthcare sector. In the subsequent section, we present the theoretical arguments in support of our hypotheses and propose the conceptual model.

2. Literature Review and Hypothesis Development

2.1 Perceived Organizational Support and Job satisfaction

Deriving its roots in organizational support theory, POS is termed as the general belief among employees concerning to the organization values, their contributions, and about their well- being. (Eisenberger, Huntington, Hutchison & Sowa, 1986). Research on POS has demonstrated favourable results on an individual as well as on organization. Perception of favourable support culminates in employees experiencing psychological well-being and positive feelings towards their work and organization (Eisenberger & Stinglhamber, 2011). Employees who believe that their organization value their contributions and is concerned about their welfare tend to reciprocate by performing their jobs well (Shore and Wayne, 1993). It meets the psychogenic needs of the employees and contributes to overall job satisfaction by conveying to employees that help and support are always available (Eisenberger and Rhoades, 2002; Casimir et al., 2014).

Job satisfaction is simply how people feel about their jobs and different aspects of their jobs. It is the extent to which people like (satisfaction) or dislike (dissatisfaction) their jobs (Spector, 1997). Both job satisfaction and dissatisfaction are a function of the perceived relationship between what one wants from one's job and how one perceive it (Locke, 1969). Job satisfaction is affected by many factors and the perception of organizational support has a predictive effect on it. Studies have shown a positive relationship between POS and job satisfaction (Shore & Tetrick, 1991; Rhoades and Eisenberger, 2002; Hongvichit, 2015). Empirical research on nursing too has found a positive relationship between POS and job satisfaction (Al-Hussami, 2008; Burke, 2003; Laschinger, Purdy, Cho, & Almost, 2006; Filipova, 2011; Poulose and Sudarsan, 2014; Shao, Zhang, & Chen, 2016). Therefore, in line with the previous research, we hypothesize;

Hypothesis 1: Perceived organizational support has a significant and positive relationship with job satisfaction.

NMIMS
Management Review
ISSN: 0971-1023
Volume XXIX
Issue-3 | July 2021

2.2 Perceived Organizational Support and Work -life balance

According to Poulose and Sudarsan (2014), the balancing act of an individual between the organization and personal life is termed as Work- life balance (WLB) or work-family balance. Work- life balance is positively associated with one's quality of life and overall well-being (Greenhaus, Collins and Shaw, 2003). Employee's perception of organizational support also predicts many work and family outcomes such as reduced role conflict, higher job satisfaction, and reduced turnover intentions. (Greenglass et al., 2001 & Garret et al., 2001). A lot of research is focused on the need of creating a proper work environment for nurses. However not much is known about the influence of POS on overall work- life balance about nurses working in hospitals as their work involves high mental as well as physical demands owing to excessive workload arising out of lean workforce in hospitals often requiring night shifts and forfeiture of normal holidays (Greenglass, Burke, & Fiksenbaum, 2001; Garret and McDaniel, 2001; McCarthy et al., 2013). Also, explicit work- life balance policies may or may not exist for nurses in the place of their work (hospitals) considering the demanding nature of their work. Thus, it could be argued that the overall perception of organizational support in terms of recognizing their contribution, care, and concern shown towards them (Eisenberger et al., 1986) may enable the nurses to balance their work and family responsibilities effectively. Therefore, we hypothesize;

Hypothesis 2: Perceived organizational support has a significant and positive relationship with work- life balance

2.3 Work- life balance and Job satisfaction

Clark (2001) defines WLB as satisfaction and good functioning at work and home with a minimum of role conflict. Considering the dual role of women in Indian society on the family and work front, WLB has become a major concern for women employees in today's scenario as extended work hours in the organization constraints their productivity and time meant to be devoted at the family front (Vasumathi, 2018). Research has found that WLB of employees increases various employee and organizational- related job outcomes (Sirgy and Lee, 2017) including job satisfaction. The same is equally true for female nurses who represent the largest group of workforce engaged in patient care. Nurses have to work in a challenging and emotionally demanding condition along with physically demanding working conditions, such as weekend work, work shifts, and high workload (Van der Heijden, Demerouti, & Bakker, 2008) which makes them more prone to work-family conflict (Yildirim and Aycan, 2008).

Most research on work- life balance has focussed on the effect of WLB on outcome variables such as job attitudes, work performance, productivity, lateness, absenteeism, and turnover (Konrad and Mangel, 2000; Anderson, Coffey, & Byerly, 2002;

NMIMS
Management Review
ISSN: 0971-1023
Volume XXIX
Issue-3 | July 2021

Behson, 2005; Ahmad, 2008; Cohen & Liani, 2009). However, studies focussing on employees' job satisfaction with work- life balance on female nurses are few and far between. Also work- life balance may or may not guarantee job satisfaction (Kim & Ryu, 2017).Considering this dichotomy over the effect of work- life balance on job satisfaction, we hypothesize;

Hypothesis 3: Work- life balance has a significant and positive relationship with job satisfaction.

2.4 Work-life balance as a mediator between Perceived Organizational Support and Work- life balance

Research has demonstrated that work- life balance leads to increased job satisfaction, health satisfaction, family satisfaction, and overall life satisfaction (Allen, Herst, Bruck, & Sutton, 2000; Keyes, 2002; Marks & MacDermid, 1996). Joseph and Lee (2017) in an integrative review on Work-life balance have identified antecedents and consequences of WLB on employee and organizational outcomes. The authors have highlighted the significance of the support system in predicting job satisfaction by assisting the employees to manage work and life demands in a better way. Further, literature on WLB, anchoring on organizational support theory (Eisenberger et al., 1986) have underscored the importance of working conditions, work environment, managerial support, work-life initiatives, and other organizational attributes in enabling the employees to manage their work and non-work demands (Casico, 2000; Gupta et al., 2015; Thomas & Ganster, 1995; Allen, 2001; Murphy and Zagorski, 2005; McCarthy et al., 2010; Brannen & Lewis, 2000). However, barring few studies (McCarthy et al., 2013 & Amazue & Onyishi, 2016), very limited research has explained the influence of general perception of support i.e., POS and WLB in the area of nursing. Casper and Buffardi (2004) and Joseph and Lee (2017) through their findings have predicted the interrelationship between POS, WLB and JS. However, very little is known on the impact of POS on job satisfaction through the mediating role of WLB in the nursing context. Therefore, in line with previous research we hypothesize;

Hypothesis 4: Work-life balance mediates the relationship of perceived organizational support and job satisfaction

NMIMS
Management Review
ISSN: 0971-1023
Volume XXIX
Issue-3 | July 2021

Figure 1: Conceptual Model

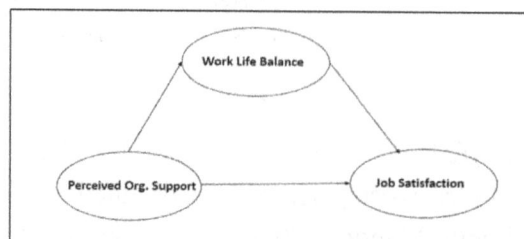

3. Research Methodology

3.1 Sample

Using the convenience sampling technique, we collected data from female nurses working in private hospitals in Mumbai over a span of four months (July, 2019 to October, 2019). The convenience sampling technique was used because of two reasons. Firstly, it was difficult to adopt probability methods of sampling because many hospitals refused to participate in the study. Secondly, Mumbai is geographically big enough with many private hospitals in different localities.

A total of 40 hospitals were visited from 13 different locations in Mumbai. Responses were collected from 250 nurses out of which 214 responses were considered fit for further analysis. Prior permission was sought from hospital administrators before collecting the responses of nurses. Questionnaires were given only to those nurses who consented to participate in the study. The purpose of the research was conveyed to the hospital administrators and the nurses at the beginning. The nurses were assured about the confidentiality and anonymity of their responses. The demographic details of the respondents are presented in table 1 given below.

Table 1: Demographic characteristics of nurses

		Frequency	Percentage %	Cumulative %
Age				
	20 to 30 years	139	65	65
	31 to 40 years	51	23.8	88.8
	41 to 50 years	17	7.9	96.7
	Above 50 years	7	3.3	100
Marital Status				
	Unmarried	111	51.9	51.9
	Married	98	45.8	97.7
	Divorcee	1	0.5	98.1
	Widow	4	1.9	100
Education				
	B.Sc Nursing	24	11.2	11.2
	M.Sc Nursing	16	7.5	18.7
	GNM	56	26.2	44.9
	ANM	90	42.1	86.9
	Others	28	13.1	100

NMIMS
NMIMS
Management Review
ISSN: 0971-1023
Volume XXIX
Issue-3 | July 2021

Experience				
	Less than 1 year	40	18.7	18.7
	2 to 5 years	106	49.5	68.2
	6 to 10 years	35	16.4	84.6
	More than 10 years	33	15.4	100
Working Status				
	Part time	13	6.1	6.1
	Full time	201	93.9	100
Working hours				
	Less than 8 hours	61	28.5	28.5
	8 to 10 hours	129	60.3	88.8
	10 to 12 hours	24	11.2	100

3.2 Measures

We used validated scales in literature to measure the constructs of perceived organizational support, work- life balance, and job satisfaction. All the constructs were measured on a five-point Likert scale ranging from Strongly Disagree (1) to Strongly Agree (5). The responses were self-reported by the nurses.

Perceived organizational support was measured through eight- item scale developed by Eisenberger et al. (1986). The sample item of the scale was; the organization values and contribution to its well-being.

Job satisfaction was measured through a 10-item generic job satisfaction scale developed by Macdonald and MacIntyre (1997). A sample item of the scale was; I receive recognition for a job well done.

Work- life balance was measured using a four- item scale developed by Brough et al. (2009). A sample item of the scale was; I currently have a good balance between the time I spend at work and the time I have available for non-work activities.

The reliability of the scales was assessed using Cronbach's alpha, a measure of internal consistency. The overall reliability for all the 22 items used in the study is 0.841 which is excellent.

4. Results

Statistical analysis was performed using IBM SPSS version 22. Hierarchical regression analysis techniques were used to test hypotheses 1, 2 and 3. Hypothesis 4 i.e., Mediation was tested using PROCESS macro plug- in for SPSS that is most

NMIMS
Management Review
ISSN: 0971-1023
Volume XXIX
Issue-3 | July 2021

popularly used in social sciences for observed variable mediation, moderation, and conditional process analysis (Hayes, 2013). We further validated the findings of mediation using Sobel test.

Perceived organizational support was found to be positively correlated with job satisfaction (r=0.533). Similarly, the correlation coefficient (r=0.314) was found to be positive between job satisfaction and work-life balance, whereas perceived organizational support and work- life balance too were found to be positively correlated (r=0.257). The alpha values for job satisfaction, perceived organizational support and work life balance were 0.814, 0.710 and 0.656 respectively. The alpha values for job satisfaction, perceived organizational support is found to be higher than the recommended value of 0.7 (Hair Jr, Anderson, Tatham, & Black, 1995). However, we found a relatively lower alpha value for work- life balance and this is acceptable in line with few previous studies on scale reliabilities (Nunnally, 1967, Aron and Aron, 1999; Hair Jr, Black, Babin, Anderson, & Tatham, 2006).

The results of descriptive statistics, scale reliability, and correlation are presented in Table 2.

Table 2: Descriptive statistics, Cronbach alpha & correlation coefficient.

Constructs	Mean	SD	α	POS	WLB	JS
Perceived Org. Support (POS)	3.749	0.536	0.710	1		
Work Life Balance (WLB)	3.690	0.633	0.656	0.257**	1	
Job Satisfaction (JS)	4.048	0.480	0.814	0.533**	0.314**	1

Notes: SD – Standard deviation; **α – Cronbach Alpha, ** Pearson's product moment correlation coefficient significant at p < 0.01**

4.1 Hierarchical Regression Analysis:

We tested three models based on our hypothesis. In model 1, job satisfaction was regressed on perceived organizational support. The results were found to be significant (β=0.533, F=83.928, p<0.001), thus providing evidence in support of our hypothesis 1 i.e., perceived organizational support has a significant and positive relationship with job satisfaction. Figure 2 presents the direct effect of POS on JS.

Figure 2: Path relationship of perceived organizational support and job satisfaction (*** p<0.001)

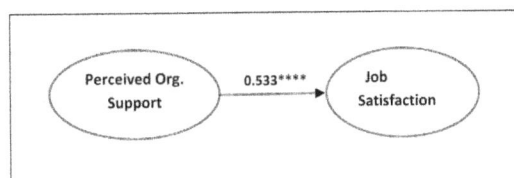

NMIMS
Deemed to be UNIVERSITY

**NMIMS
Management Review**
ISSN: 0971-1023
Volume XXIX
Issue-3 | July 2021

In model 2, we regressed, work- life balance on perceived organizational support. The results were found to be significant (β=0.257, F=15.009, p<0.001) providing evidence in support of hypothesis 2 i.e., perceived organizational support has a significant and positive relationship with work-life balance. In model 3, we regressed, job satisfaction on perceived organizational support and work- life balance to assess the total effects of both variables on the outcome variable. The results were again found to be significant (β (POS)=0.484, β (WLB)=0.189, F=48.979, p<0.001) providing evidence in support of hypothesis 3 i.e., work- life balance has a significant and positive relationship with job satisfaction. It was also found that the original effect of POS on JS as evidenced in model 1 further declined from (β=0.533) to (β =0.484) in the presence of work- life balance, thus suggesting possible mediation of WLB in the relationship of POS and JS (Baron & Kenny, 1986). Table 3 given below depicts standardised regression coefficients and other statistics related to the model, and figure 3 represents the mediation effect.

Table 3: Result of Hierarchical Regression Analysis

Constructs	Dependent Variable		
	Job Satisfaction	Work Life Balance	Job Satisfaction
	Model 1	Model 2	Model 3
Perceived Organizational Support	0.533***	0.257***	0.484***
Work Life Balance	-	-	0.189***
R^2	0.284	0.066	0.317
ΔR^2	0.284	0.066	0.033
F value	83.928***	15.009***	48.979***

*** Standardized coefficients (β) significant at p<0.001

Figure 3: Mediation effect of work life balance in the relationship of perceived organizational support and job satisfaction (*p<0.001)**

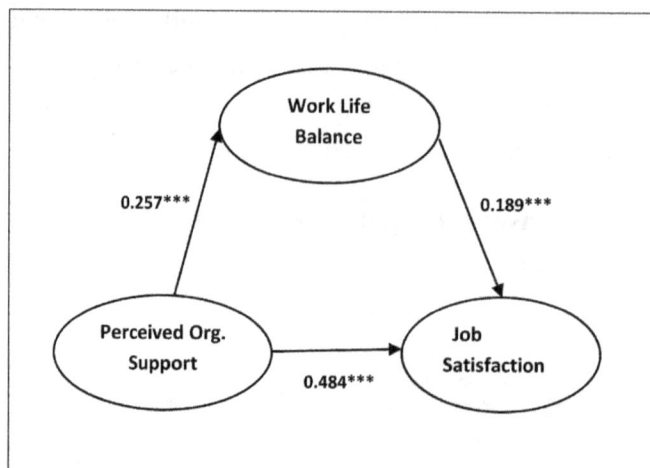

NMIMS
Management Review
ISSN: 0971-1023
Volume XXIX
Issue-3 | July 2021

104

Furthermore, we tested the possible mediation of WLB as indicated in hierarchical regression analysis using PROCESS macro plug-in (Hayes, 2013) and Sobel test. Mediation results derived from the PROCESS macro plug-in with a bootstrap sample size of 10,000 showed that work- life balance mediated the relationship of POS and JS. Sobel's test for indirect effect too was found to be significant (Sobel t = 2.491, p< 0.05). This provided evidence in support of our conceptual model and hypothesis 4 i.e., work-life balance mediates the relationship of perceived organizational support and work-life balance. The results of mediation with effect size and Sobel test are given in Table 4.

Table 4: Mediation results

Mediation	Effect	Boot SE	Boot LLCI	Boot ULCI	Sobel test
POS > WLB > JS	0.046	0.022	0.013	0.102	2.491*

*significant at p<0.05

5. Discussion

Female nurses occupy a centre stage in the delivery of nursing services in the healthcare scenario. They play a quintessential role in patient care as they spend considerable time looking after their needs and even assist doctors on a routine basis. Therefore, challenges associated with the nursing profession are varied and have a potential impact on their satisfaction level which has resulted in increased attrition particularly among female nurses. Our findings adequately validate the role of organizational support theory in influencing an important individual outcome i.e., job satisfaction of nurses in the Indian healthcare space. Hospital administrators in this regard need to be mindful of ensuring an adequate support system to nurses so that they in term experience a positive perception of organizational support. Higher levels of support will surely prevent attrition by enhancing satisfaction levels with the job as they would be more dependent on their organization for their personal and professional needs.

Furthermore, female nurses represent the majority workforce in hospitals and outnumber men nursing staff in the Indian healthcare system. Additionally, given the peculiar characteristic of women in Indian society, they perform twin roles as a homemaker on the family front and as caregivers in hospitals. Therefore, it is practicable to expect issues of work-life balance with them not much in common with their male counterparts. Poor perception of organizational support and inability to handle work and family demands results in dissatisfaction. Hence, our conceptualization of the theoretical model (POS – WLB – JS Model) is based on peculiarities that are realistic for female nurses in the Indian healthcare context. Our study throws light on the process that leads to satisfaction of nurses with their job through the mediating role of work-life balance in the relationship of POS and JS. Our study equitably demonstrates

NMIMS
NMIMS
Management Review
ISSN: 0971-1023
Volume XXIX
Issue-3 | July 2021

that nurses' perception of organizational support at the work place has a cascading impact on their subjective assessment of balancing multifarious roles at the personal and organizational level popularly referred to as work- life balance (Haar et al., 2014 & Greenhaus & Allen, 2011).

Lastly, this study contributes to the existing literature in nursing and organizational support in several ways. Firstly, we use the distal support at the organizational level which encompasses a general level of support (McCarthy et al., 2013) which nurses experience in their workplaces and is operationalized as perceived organizational support. In addition, drawing from the organizational support theory, we make a distinction between specific support and overall support that exists in the workplace. We found that such distal support as perceived by nurses has a significant and positive relationship with job satisfaction and work-life balance. In addition, we also found distal support to be positively related to work-life balance. Earlier studies have linked work-life balance to various work-life initiatives (specific support) which the organization had for their employees. Studies linking distal (general support) to work life balance are very limited. This is one of the main contributions of the study as explicit work-life balance policies may or may not exist for nurses considering the very demanding nature of their work. Thus, we argue that the overall perception of organizational support in terms of recognizing their contribution, care, and concern shown towards them (Eisenberger et al., 1986) will enable the nurses to balance their work and family responsibilities effectively. Further, in line with our findings, we expect that higher levels of organizational support even though distal as perceived by nurses would foster better work-life balance which in turn would enhance their overall job satisfaction.

6. Implications of the Study

The study explores the relationship between perceived organizational support and job satisfaction through the mediating role of work-life balance. POS and WLB are significant predictors in enhancing the satisfaction level of nurses in private hospitals. This study assumes significance for healthcare administrators, doctors, and practitioners who have a pivotal role to play in the delivery of healthcare services through nurses by providing better support systems at the workplace in terms of supervision, proper working environment, rewards and recognition, decent salary. Work-life balance has an equally important role to play in enhancing the satisfaction level of nurses as females have a dual role to perform unlike men. Work- life initiatives for nurses such as flexible timings, work sharing, proper leave policies, supervisory support etc. would go a long way in enhancing their overall satisfaction and reducing attritions. Proper support systems at hospitals for females can help them to take care of their responsibilities at the home and organizational front systematically.

NMIMS
Management Review
ISSN: 0971-1023
Volume XXIX
Issue-3 | July 2021

7. Limitations

Despite the empirical nature of the study and its usefulness, it is not free from limitations. The first limitation is concerning our sample and the sampling technique. Our research is exclusively centred on understanding the constructs of perceived support, work- life balance, and job satisfaction as female nurses are only given the dominance of the female workforce in the nursing profession. Future research may involve male counterparts to female nurses in the healthcare space. This would help in exploring the comparative understanding of the important phenomenon covered in our study. In addition, the findings of the study are based on convenience sampling, a non-probability method, which requires readers to exercise a plausible degree of caution as far as the generalizability of the study is concerned. The second limitation concerning the nature of our research data is cross-sectional in nature. Thirdly, we suggest future researchers' measure organizational support in terms of work-life balance separately and assess its influence on the relationship of work-life balance and job satisfaction. This would possibly explain additional variance in the conceptual model. Researchers may try inclusion of other antecedents to job satisfaction at an individual and organizational level as mediators and moderators in our proposed theoretical framework. Despite limitations in our study, we expect it to be useful for readers, researchers, and practitioners in understanding the association of three crucial constructs for female nurses in the Indian healthcare industry.

8. Conclusion

Female nurses working in hospitals are the backbone of the healthcare system in India. It is difficult to imagine hospitals without them. Therefore, organizational support, work- life balance, and job satisfaction are important areas where considerable attention is warranted. Given the prevalence of high attrition rates in nursing, it becomes imperative that adequate work- life balance support should be provided to them. This would increase their perception of support at the workplace which in turn would enable them to be satisfied with their jobs through work- life balance. The study explains the process by which the job satisfaction level of nurses can be enhanced through greater organizational support and work-life balance. Our findings suggest that work-life balance mediates the relationship between perceived organizational support and job satisfaction. Even distal perception of support influences job satisfaction through work-life balance. Hence, it is suggested that they are provided organizational support at work such as a decent work environment, rewards and recognition, social and moral support from supervisors, adequate leaves, and timely breaks during work hours so that they experience balance and satisfaction on the job and family front.

NMIMS
Management Review
ISSN: 0971-1023
Volume XXIX
Issue-3 | July 2021

References

Abou Hashish, E. A. (2017). Relationship between ethical work climate and nurses' perception of organizational support, commitment, job satisfaction and turnover intent. *Nursing Ethics*, 24 (2), 151-166.

Ahmad, A. (2008). Direct and indirect effects of work-family conflict on job performance. *The Journal of International Management Studies*, Vol 3, No 2, 176-180.

Aiken, L. H., Clarke, S. P., Sloane, D. M., Sochalski, J., & Silber, J. H. (2002). Hospital nurse staffing and patient mortality, nurse burnout, and job dissatisfaction. *JAMA* 288 (16), 1987-1993.

Allen, T. D., Herst, D. E., Bruck, C. S., & Sutton, M. (2000). Consequences associated with work to family conflict: a review and agenda for future research. *Journal of Occupational Health,* Vol 5, No 2, 278-308.

Alotaibi, J., Paliadelis, P. S., & Valenzuela, F. R. (2016). Factors that affect the job satisfaction of Saudi Arabian Nurses. *Journal Of Nursing Management*, 275-282.

Amazue, L. O., & Onyishi, I. E. (2015). Stress Coping Strategies, Perceived Organizational Support and Marital Status as Predictors of Work–Life Balance among Nigerian Bank Employees. *Social Indicators Research*.

Anderson, S. E., B S, C., & R T, B. (2002). Formal organizational initiatives and informal workplace practices: Link to work-family conflict and job-related outcomes. *Journal of Management,* 787-810.

Aron, A., & Aron, E. (1999). Statistics for psychology (2 ed.). *Upper Saddle River, NJ: Prentice Hall.*

Baron, R. M., & Kenny, D. A. (1986). The Moderator-Mediator Variable Distinction in Social Psychological Research: Conceptual, Strategic, and Statistical Considerations. *Journal of Personality and Social Psychology*, 1173-1182.

Brough, P., Timms, C., O'Driscoll, M., Kalliath, T., Siu, O.-L., Sit, C., & Lo, D. (2014). Work-life balance: a longitudinal evaluation of a new measure across Australia and New Zealand workers. *The International Journal of Human Resource Management.*

Burke, R. J. (2003). Nursing staff attitudes following restructuring: The role of perceived organizational support, restructuring processes, and stressors. *International Journal of Sociology and Social Policy,* 23(8/9), 129-157.

Cascio, W. F. (2000). Costing human resources: The financial impact of behaviour in organization (4th ed). Cincinnati, OH: Southwestern.

Casimir, G., Ngee Keith Ng, Y., Yuan Wang, K., & Ooi, G. (2014). The relationships amongst leader-member exchange, perceived organizational support, affective commitment, and in-role performance. *Leadership & Organizational Development Journal*, 366-385.

Casper, W. J., & Buffardi, L. C. (2004). Work-life benefits and Job Pursuit Intentions: The role of anticipated organisational support. *Journal of Vocational Behaviour*, 88,4, 605-619.

Cavanagh, S. J. (1992). Job satisfaction of nursing staff working in hospitals. *Journal of Advanced Nursing,* 17, 704-711.

Chang, C. S. (2015). Moderating Effects of Nurses' Organizational Support on the Relationship Between Job Satisfaction and Organizational Commitment. *Western Journal of Nursing Research,* 37 (6), 724-745.

Cohen, A., & Liani, E. (2009). Work family conflict among female nurses in Israeli hospitals. *Personnel Review*, Vol 38, No 2, 124-141.

Demerouti, E., Bakker, A. B., & Bulters, A. J. (2005). The loss spiral of work pressure, work-home interference, and exhaustion: reciprocal relations in a three-wave study. *Journal of Vocational Behaviour,* 64(1), 131-149.

Eisenberger, R., & Stinglhamber, F. (2011). Perceived Organizational Support: Fostering Enthusiastic and Productive Employees. *American Psychological Association Books*, Washington.

Eisenberger, R., Huntington, R., Hutchison, S., & Sowa, D. (1986). Perceived Organizational Support. *Journal of Applied Psychology,*71, 500-507.

Eisenberger, R., Shanock, L. R., & Wen, X. (2019). Perceived Organizational Support: Why Caring About Employees Counts. *Annual Review of Organizational Psychology and Organizational Behaviour.*

FICCI. (August,2016). Nursing reforms paradigm shift for a bright future. Retrieved from http://ficci.in/spdocument/20756/FICCI_heal-Report_Final-27-08-2016.pdf

Filippova, A. A. (2011). Relationships among ethical climates, perceived organizational support, and intent to leave for licensed nurses in skilled nursing facilities. *Journal of Applied Gerontology,* 1-23.

Gangadhraiah, H., Nardev, G., & Reddy, M. (1990). Nurses job satisfaction in mental health and neuro-science setting. *Nursing Journal of India*, 201-204.

Garret, D. K., & McDaniel, A. M. (2001). A new look at nurse burnout: the effects of environmental uncertainty and social climate. *Journal of Nursing Administration*, Vol.31, 91-96.

Gill, R. (2011). Nursing shortage in India with special reference to international migration of nurses. *Social Medicine*, 52-59.

Gillet, N., Colombat, P., Michinov, E., Pronost, A. M., & Fouquereau, E. (2013). Procedural justice, supervisor autonomy support, work satisfaction, organizational identification, and job performance: the mediating role of need satisfaction and perceived organizational support. *Journal of Advanced Nursing.*

Greenglass, E. R., Burke, R. J., & Fiksenbaum, L. (2001). Workload and burnout in nurses.

NMIMS
Management Review
ISSN: 0971-1023
Volume XXIX
Issue-3 | July 2021

Journal of Community and Applied Social Psychology, Vol 11, 211-215.

Greenhaus, J. H., & Beutell, N. J. (1985). Sources of conflict between work and family roles. *Academy of Management Review*, 10, 76-88.

Greenhaus, J. H., Collins, K. M., & Shaw, J. D. (2003). The relation between work-family balance and quality of life. *Journal of Vocational Behaviour*, 63, 510-531.

Greenhaus, J., & Allen, T. (2011). Work-family balance: A review and extension of the literature., *Handbook of occupational health psychology (2nd edition)*. Washington, DC: American Psychological Association.

Gupta, V., Agarwal, U. A., & Khatri, N. (2016). The relationships between perceived organizational support, affective commitment, psychological contract breach, organizational citizenship behaviour and work engagement. *Journal of Advanced Nursing*.

Haar, J.M., Russo, M., Sune, A. & Ollier-Malaterre, A. (2014). Outcomes of work-life balance on job satisfaction, life satisfaction and mental health: a study across seven cultures, *Journal of Vocational Behaviour*, Vol.85, No 3

Hair Jr, J. F., Anderson, R. E., Tatham, R. L., & Black, W. (1995). *Multivariate data analysis with readings*. New York: Macmillan.

Hair Jr, J. F., Black, W. C., Babin, B. J., Anderson, R. E., & Tatham, R. L. (2006). *Multivariate data analysis*. Printice Hall Pearson Education.

Han, R. M., Carter, P., & Champion, J. D. (2018). Relationships among factors affecting advanced practice registered nurses' job satisfaction and intent to leave: A systematic review. *Journal of the American Association of Nurse Practitioners*, Vol 30, No 2.

Hayes, A. F. (2013). Methodology in Social Sciences. Introduction to mediation, moderation, and conditional process analysis: A regression-based approach. Guilford Press.

Hongvichit, S. (2015). A review of the research on perceived organizational support. *International Business Research*, 10.

Hosseinabadi Bagheri, M., Siavash, E., Narges, K., Omran, A., Gholiani, H., Galeshi, M., & Samaei, S. E. (2018). Evaluating the relationship between job stress and job satisfaction among female nurses in Babol: An application of structural equation modelling. *Health Promotion Perspectives*, 102-108.

Johnson, S. E., Judith, G., & Maben, J. (2014). A suitable job? A qualitative study of becoming a nurse in the context of a globalizing profession in India. *International Journal of Nursing Studies*, 734-743.

Joseph Sirgy, M., & Lee, D.-J. (2017). Work life balance: An Integrative Review. *Applied Research in Quality of Life*.

Keyes, C. L. (2002). The mental health continuum: from languishing to flourishing in life. *Journal of Health and Social Behaviour*,43, 207-222.

NMIMS
Management Review
ISSN: 0971-1023
Volume XXIX
Issue-3 | July 2021

Kim, S. J., & Ryu, S. (2017). Employee satisfaction with work-life balance policies and organization commitment: A Philippine Study. *Public Administration and Development.*

Konrad, A. M., & Mangel, R. (2000). The impact of work-life programs on firm productivity. *Strategic Management Journal,* Vol 21, No 12, 1225-1237.

Kuaru, T. (1994). Job satisfaction and burnout among nurses in a metropolitan hospital in Papua New Guinea. *South Pacific Journal of Psychology,* 7, 10-17.

Kumar, P., Dass, M., & Topaloglu, O. (2014). Understanding the drivers of job satisfaction of frontline service employees: learning from 'lost employees'. *Journal of Service Research* 17(4), 367-380.

Kurtessis, J. N., Eisenberger, R., Ford, M. T., Buffardi, L. C., Stewart, K. A., & Adis, C. S. (2015). Perceived Organizational Support: A meta-analytic evaluation of organizational support theory. *Journal of Management,* Vol.XX, No.X, 1-31.

Kwak, C., Chung, B. Y., Xu, Y., & Eun-Jung, C. (2010). Relationship of job satisfaction with perceived organizational support and quality care among South Korean nurses: A questionnaire survey. *International Journal of Nursing Studies,* 1292-1298.

Laschinger, H. K., Purdy, N., Cho, J., & Almost, J. (2006). Antecedents and consequences of nurse managers' perceptions of organizational support. *Nursing Economics,* 24(1), 20-29.

Li, X., Zhang, Y., Yan, D., Wen, F., & Zhang, Y. (2020). Nurses' intention to stay: The impact of perceived organizational support, job control and job satisfaction. *Journal of Advanced Nursing.*

Locke, E. A. (1969). What is Job Satisfaction. *Organizational and Human Performance,* 309-336.

Lu, H., Zhao, Y., & Alison, W. (2019). Job satisfaction among hospital nurses: A literature review. *International Journal of Nursing Studies,* 94, 21-31.

Lum, L., Kervin, J., Clark, K., Reid, F., & and Sirola, W. (1998). Explaining nursing turnover intent: job satisfaction, pay satisfaction, or organizational commitment? *Journal of Organizational Behaviour,* 305-320.

Macdonald, S., & MacIntyre, P. (1997). The Generic Job Satisfaction Scale: Scale Development and Its Correlates. *Employee Assistance Quarterly,* Vol. 13(2).

Marks, S. R., & MacDermind, S. M. (1996). Multiple roles and the self: a theory of role balance. *Journal of Marriage and the Family,* 58, 417-432.

Martin., B. (1990). A successful approach to absenteeism. *Nursing Management* 21, 45-48.

McCarthy, A., Cleveland N, J., Hunter, S., Darcy, C., & Grady, G. (2013). Employee work-life balance outcomes in Ireland: a multilevel investigation of supervisory support and perceived organizational support. *The International Journal of Human Resource Management,* 24:6, 1257-1276.

NMIMS

**NMIMS
Management Review**
ISSN: 0971-1023
Volume XXIX
Issue-3 | July 2021

McCarthy, A., Darcy, C., & Grady, G. (2010). Work–life balance policy and practice: Understanding line manager attitudes and behaviours. *Human Resource Management Review,* 20, 158–167.

McQueen, A. C. (2004). Emotional intelligence in nursing work. *Journal of Advanced Nursing,* 47(1), 101-108.

Murphy, S. E., & Zagorski, D. A. (2005). Enhancing work–family and work–life interaction: The role of management. *In D. F. Halpern & S. E. Murphy (Eds.), From work–family balance to work–family interaction. Changing the metaphor. Hilsdale, NJ: Lawrence Erlbaum Associates,* 27-47.

Murray, M. a. (1988). Nursing Morale in Toronto: An Analysis of Career, Job and Hospital Satisfaction among hospital staff nurses. *The Nursing Manpower Task Force of the hospital Council of Metropolitan Toronto, Toronto.*

Nunnally, J. C. (1967). Psychometric theory. *New York: McGraw Hill.*

Park, K. (2011). Textbook of preventive and social medicine. *Jabalpur: Banarsidas Bhanot Publishers.*

Poulose, S., & Sudarshan, N. (2017). Assessing the influence of work-life balance dimensions among nurses in the healthcare sector. *Journal of Management Development,* Vol.36 Issue 3.

Rhoades, L., & Eisenberger, R. (2002). Perceived Organizational Support: A review of the literature. *Journal of Applied Psychology,* 698-714.

Riggle, R. J., Edmondson, D. R., & Hansen, J. D. (2009). A meta-analysis of the relationship between perceived organizational support and job outcomes: 20 years of research. *Journal of Business Research,* 1027-1030.

Robert J Riggle, D. R. (October 2009). A meta-analysis of the relationship between perceived organizational support and job outcomes: 20 years of research. *Journal of Business Research,* 1027-1030.

Shao, J., Zhang, Y., & Chen, X. (2016). Influence of perceived organizational support and job involvement on job satisfaction of psychiatric nurses. *Nursing research of China,*30, 2643-2647.

Shore, L. M., & Shore, T. H. (1995). Perceived organizational support and organizational justice, (Cropanzano R. & Kacmar K.M., eds). *Organizational Politics, Justice and Support: Managing Social Climate at Work,* 149-164.

Shore, L. M., & Tetrick, L. E. (1991). A construct validity study of the survey of perceived organizational support. *Journal of Applied Psychology,* 76, 637-643.

Shore, L. M., & Wayne, S. J. (1993). Commitment and Employee Behaviour: Comparison of Affective Commitment and Continuance Commitment with Perceived Organizational Support. *Journal of Applied Psychology,* Vol 78, No-5, 774780.

NMIMS
Management Review
ISSN: 0971-1023
Volume XXIX
Issue-3 | July 2021

Sirgy, M., & Lee, D.-J. (2107). Work-Life Balance: An Integrative Review. *Applied Research Quality Life.*

Spector, P. (1997). Job Satisfaction: Application, Assessment, Causes and Consequences. *SAGE Publications, Inc, Thousand Oaks, CA.*

Thomas, L. T., & Ganster, D. (1995). Impact of family-supportive work variables on work–family conflict and strain: A control perspective. *Journal of Applied Psychology,* 80(1), 6-15.

Van Der Heijden, B., Demerouti, E., & Bakker, A. B. (2008). Work-home interference among nurses: reciprocal relationships with job demands and health. *Journal of Advanced Nursing,* Vol 62, No 5, 572-584.

Vasumathi, A. (2018). Work life balance of women employees: A literature review. *International Journal of Services and Operations Management.*

Yildirim, D., & Aycan, Z. (2008). Nurses work demands and work family conflict: A questionnaire survey, Vol 45 No 9. *International Journal of Nursing Studies,* 1366-1378.

Arun kumar Dubey is an Assistant Professor in Commerce & Management at S K Somaiya College of Arts, Science & Commerce. He can be reached at prof. arunkumard@gmail.com, His ORCID id is https://orcid.org/0000-0002-7427-8254

Dr. S Riasudeen is an Associate Professor at Department of Management Studies, School of Management, Pondicherry University. He can be reached at riasudeen. dms@pondiuni.edu.in, His ORCID id is https://orcid.org/0000-0002-3177-6333

NMIMS
NMIMS
Management Review
ISSN: 0971-1023
Volume XXIX
Issue-3 | July 2021

Black Eagle Books

www.blackeaglebooks.org
info@blackeaglebooks.org

Black Eagle Books, an independent publisher, was founded as a nonprofit organization in April, 2019. It is our mission to connect and engage the Indian diaspora and the world at large with the best of works of world literature published on a collaborative platform, with special emphasis on foregrounding Contemporary Classics and New Writing.